SUMMER PEOPLE

or

*How Nudists, Boozers and One Headless Turkey
Influenced a Boy's Life*

by

CLIFF KORRADI

Summer People

or

*How Nudists, Boozers and One Headless Turkey
Influenced a Boy's Life*

CLIFF KORRADI

PARKE | PRESS

Norfolk

Dedicated

to Robert

Summer People • Copyright © 2016 by Clifford Korradi
All rights reserved.
cliffkor@gmail.com • summerpeoplethebook.com

PUBLISHED BY
PARKE PRESS
Norfolk, Virginia
www.parkepress.com

ISBN 978-0-9843339-9-8

Library of Congress Control Number is available upon request

Printed in the United States of America

Table of Contents

The Maples • Spofford, New Hampshire

The
Maples

Spofford
New
Hampshire

Delightfully situated one mile from beautiful Lake
Spofford, ten miles from Keene, NH and
twelve miles from Brattleboro, VT. Ideal for
recreation, rest, comfort and health.
Modern improvements, telephone, electricity, baths,
beautiful large airy rooms, delicious wholesome foods,
temptingly cooked and served German-American style.
We accommodate 15 people. Rates upon request.

Marion and Fred Korradi

Phone Spofford 146 • Box 22, Spofford, NH

*This photo of The Maples, and the description of its amenities,
comes from a 1944 brochure that was used as advertising
and given to all guests.*

INTRODUCTION

or

Everything Has To Start Somewhere

IT ALL BEGAN in June of 1943. My parents, Fred and Marion Korradi of the Bronx, New York, bought The Maples in Spofford, New Hampshire. Located in the southwest corner of the state, Spofford is one of three small villages that make up the town of Chesterfield. It was a big leap for this young couple with a child less than a year old (me), and my mother's mother, Martha Scheuermann, otherwise known as Oma (that's German for grandmother), to pack up and leave the comfort and conveniences of city life and relocate to the wilds of New Hampshire.

As they explained it, friends from the Bronx moved to Spofford in the 1930s, liked it, and convinced them New York was no longer a good place to raise a family. Nazi U-boats were sinking ships off Sandy Hook, New Jersey, as well as Long Island, and soon, they figured, the Second World War would be fought in their neighborhood. So they headed for the land of maple syrup to start a new life.

The Maples was not just a rambling, 10-bedroom house with a huge kitchen and a stone fireplace in the living room; it also included 57 acres of woods made up of mostly sugar maples, a great trout stream – Partridge Brook – and a mountain named Mt. Pistareen. All of that cost them a mere $6,200, including furniture. That price really hit home when, in 1975, I bought a new Saab and took it to show my dad. I still had the price sticker on the window and he looked at it, running his finger down to the grand total, which was $6,450.

Mom and Dad relax at Coney Island in 1940 BC, (before Clifford, as they explained it). They would soon learn firsthand that running a New Hampshire inn wasn't always a day at the beach.

He shook his head and asked in astonishment if I really paid that much for a car. I tried to explain that I had a trade-in and that wasn't the real cost but he would have none of it. He just spread his arms and said, "I can't believe you would spend $6,400 for a car when your mother and I got all of this for $6,200!"

By the way, many years after they bought the place, a neighbor told them they could have gotten it for $5,000 but because they were from New York, the owner thought they had a lot of money – so the price went up.

The original plan was to raise chickens and take in summer people, something that had been done for many years by the previous owner. However, it soon became clear that this scheme would not bring in enough money. So my father found a job at the American Optical Company in Brattleboro, Vermont, where he became a precision lens grinder and worked on such diverse projects as creating optics for the military, 3-D camera lenses, and the widescreen Todd-AO camera system. He chose the night shift because it paid 10 percent more than working days. Besides, he used the days to work on the house, which always needed upkeep and repairs, and during the summer he shuttled summer people to and from the train station in Brattleboro, tended the garden, mixed drinks, washed dishes, and in general was the majordomo.

SO THAT IS HOW I GREW UP, with the strangers who shared our home from June to September for more than 15 years. They were the summer people and, in many ways, they helped shape my life. Here, for your amusement, are some of their stories.

All of the events in this book are true.
Some conversations have been reconstructed from memory
because, frankly, as a seven-year-old, I wasn't taking notes
on the tablecloth as I waited on summer people.
Also, some names have been changed.

A SUN WORSHIPER IN OUR MIDST

or

Never Let Your Mother Know You Ran Naked

Through the Poison Ivy

"I THINK ONE OF YOUR BOARDERS is a nudist," Charlie Warren said to my mother as she served him eggs and bacon one morning in the summer of 1949.

By this time, my mother and father had become unflappable vis-á-vis comments made by our guests. From heated arguments about politics to traveling salesman jokes (fueled and nurtured by adult beverages and smoky card games), they both tended to remain as cool as the cucumbers, served with Oma's special garlic, vinegar, and sour cream dressing, when it came to things said by the summer people.

I was wearing my oversized, white waiter's jacket, the one that reached below my bony seven-year-old knees, and was refreshing Charlie's ice water when he broke the news. I wasn't sure what "nudist" meant, but based on the smirk I saw plastered across his face, I suspected it was something that kids weren't supposed to know about. I had seen the same smirk when the traveling salesman jokes were told during the late-night pinochle playoffs.

"Shhhh," Helen, Charlie's wife, said as she poked his arm.

"I'm only telling you what I saw, and I saw Mrs. Milligan bare-ass naked in the woods this morning," he maintained as he pulled away from his wife's digital jabbing.

"You did not," she insisted. "Now, be quiet!"

But he would not be quiet. There's something about someone seeing someone else naked that makes the first someone want to talk about it. "I know a nudist when I see one and I saw one about thirty minutes ago!"

"Little pitchers have big ears," my mother said, tilting her head in my direction. Then, looking at me, she smiled and pointed toward the kitchen. "Clifford, see if the toast is ready."

Who was she trying to kid? Her kid, that's who. I had already served the toast and, judging by the debris field of crumbs on the table, Charlie had consumed three or four slices.

I wanted to say, "Mom, we can't make toast fast enough to fill the hole in this guy's face. Look at the table; it's like an explosion in a crouton factory." Nevertheless, when my mom pointed toward a distant place, with directions to travel in that general direction, it was wise to do so. Failure could result in the dreaded lecture, the double-dreaded smack on the pants or the most diabolical of all the dreads, no new comic books.

So I hoisted my water pitcher with its handle that was way larger than my ears, including the left one that stuck out just like Bing Crosby's, and retreated to the kitchen.

"Mom says Mr. Warren needs more toast," I told my father who was alternating between washing dishes and feeding four toasters.

"What does he think this is, a bakery?" Dad said as he quickly wiped his soapy hands on a towel and dealt six slices of white bread as fast as a dealer would pass out cards from a fresh deck. He did both with ease, by the way.

Breakfast was a busy time in The Maples' kitchen. Between scrambling, poaching, soft boiling and flipping eggs on the massive, six-burner, cast iron stove, Oma fried bacon and ham slices while starting to prepare the noontime dinner, which was just a few hours away. She might be trussing a chicken, trimming a pot roast, or inserting slivers of fresh garlic into a yard-long loin of pork. All this while muttering in German and telling my mother what fresh things she needed from the garden.

Into this orchestrated confusion Mom walked, carrying a tray of egg-streaked dishes and lipstick-tattooed coffee cups. "You won't believe what Charlie Warren just told me," she said to my old man who stacked the warm toast on a plate and handed it to me. "Tell him we're out of bread," Dad instructed as he ushered me toward the dining room. But I wanted to hear what Mom was going to say. She leaned toward him and whispered something. All I could hear was that word, "nudist." They both looked at me and said nothing. Boy, that must have been some word. Now two people didn't want me to hear it. Finally, the old man broke the silence. "He's nuts," he roared with a loud laugh and went back to the pile of dishes in the sink.

"Vot's zo funny?" Oma asked in her thick German accent.

"Just something Charlie thought he saw. It's nothing important," Mom said as she hung up her apron and started to put the wet towels in the laundry.

"I never get za joak," Oma sighed hopelessly as she went back to her cooking.

"Marion, I'm sorry for what just happened. Sometimes I think Charlie just says things to shock people." It was Mrs. Warren and she was standing in the doorway that separated the dining room from the kitchen. "Last month he told my father he'd seen Adolph Hitler washing windows on Fifth Avenue. I though Poppa was going to have a heart attack and he insisted I immediately call J. Edgar Hoover and let him know. Charlie was only kidding, of course, but people always take him so seriously."

"Well, the guy washing windows did look a little like Hitler." Charlie now joined his wife in the doorway. "But what I saw this morning looked a whole lot like that Mrs. Milligan and she didn't have a stitch on. She was just going into the woods at the far end of the field, down by the brook."

"Leave it to you to count stitches," his wife said with a nasty tone. "Besides, what were you doing out looking for naked women this morning?"

This was getting interesting and I got on my hands and knees and sat under the table in the middle of the room. That way I would be out of sight but could hear everything. It's a move that had worked many times before, and on more than one occasion gave me the heads-up on great birthday presents and really cool Christmas gifts.

"Oma, the eggs were zar-goot," Charlie said with a laugh as he waved to my grandmother.

"Danka," she replied and turned back to the big stove.

"I'm sure you saw Mrs. Milligan, she's always up early and likes to wade in the brook," Mom tried to reason, "And maybe she was wearing a brown shirt and shorts."

Now, let me give you some background information about Mrs. Milligan. She was a small, dark-skinned woman of undetermined age and racial background. Dad once described her as looking like Mahatma Gandhi's twin sister, so that's why Mom's portrayal of her wearing brown clothing as the possible basis for Charlie's naked-eye sighting made perfect sense. Mrs. Milligan also spoke with a distinct Austrian accent and lived in the Greenwich Village section of New York City where, presumably, her eccentricities, such as being an alleged "sun worshiper," were not only accepted – they were probably encouraged and welcomed. Who knew, possibly even with open arms and eyes. One thing we did know: she had been coming to our place for several years and was always accompanied by her daughter, Sonya, who was three years my senior.

Sonya Milligan could best be described as a tomboy. She'd out-run, out-swim, out-climb, out-pitch, out-hit, and out-spit any man or boy in the house. Her goal in life was to become the first girl shortstop for the New York Giants.

Alvin Dark, the scrappy Giants' shortstop, was her hero but his days were numbered, if she had anything to say about it. However, as I saw it, her true God-given gift was pure show biz. It came to light when she cleared out the entire dining room by announcing she could swallow a whole glass of milk in one gulp and make it come out of her nose, without gagging – and then did it. All the while her mother was reading *The New York Times*, oblivious to the show-stopping act going on across the table from her. Sonya's legitimate talent, however, involved the violin. She attended the prestigious Juilliard School of Music in

After a hard night of cocktails, cards and chit-chat, or one of Oma's dinners, most summer people assumed this pose.

New York, and as much of a milk-spewing phenomenon as she was, she ranked as a genuine genius when it came to playing the violin – and woe betide anyone who called her instrument a fiddle. She would immediately challenge the offender to the combat of their choice including, but not limited to, arm wrestling, boxing, judo or tree climbing. If the challengee was foolish enough to accept, defeat was inevitable and swift. Sonya didn't fiddle around when it came to defending her art and her instrument.

While Sonya obviously had a first name, no one knew her mother's. She was just, Mrs. Milligan. Keep in mind that at this time, there were no credit cards and my father, in his role of the innkeeper, didn't like checks and so insisted on being paid in cash, which Mrs. Milligan always did. When her funds were running low, she placed a long-distance collect call to a merchant marine union headquarters somewhere in New

15

York, and within two days, her husband, a ship's captain, always wired more money. There was speculation among some that he probably was glad to have her in New Hampshire, and would gladly pay any amount to keep it that way. At least that's how the summer people saw it.

Talk of Mrs. Milligan's alleged proclivity for skipping through the woods "au naturel" soon faded like last summer's tan. Mrs. Warren told her husband to stop spreading rumors and apparently she had the power of persuasion because Charlie didn't say another word about it.

I didn't think about the "nudist" word after that morning because I had other things on my mind, namely work. My typical day during the summer was chore-driven. Up at 6:30 a.m. when Mom, Dad, and Oma got up. We had a quick breakfast before setting the tables on the dining porch for the guests who were served between 8:00 and 9:00. As the sleepy company shuffled in (those late-night pinochle/poker/ canasta games fueled with boilermakers and highballs had a way of taking their toll), the first request was always a cup of Mom's strong coffee, which she would serve while I filled the water glasses. Because some of our guests just wanted coffee before going out to relax and trod the New Hampshire hills, the dining porch wasn't as full as at dinnertime.

When the last breakfast guest left I cleared the tables, wiping away the crumbs and picking up anything that might have hit the floor. In the off-season my dog, Rover, was more than willing to assist in the floor cleaning, but it was not considered good form or accepted hygiene to use a furry vacuum cleaner around the paying clientele. If the old man was still doing dishes, I wiped and stacked what was left. Next came going to the garden to pick whatever fresh vegetable Oma wanted to serve with dinner.

The main meal of the day was served at noon and never failed to be a winner. Oma used all of her talents as a German chef and I was kept very busy bussing tables and delivering steaming bowls of fresh vegetables and platters of savory meats. After dessert, my mother's specialty, the tables were cleared, the Korradi family ate lunch, and the dishes were done.

A full belly usually resulted in guests nodding off to sleep on the cool screened porch or under the massive maple tree on the lawn. Oma always took a nap, too, and my dad tried to get in a few winks before heading off for work. Mom would spend the afternoons making beds, straightening up the rooms or doing laundry. My afternoons were free time and if any of the guests wanted to go for a swim in Spofford Lake, I was always more than willing to show the way and point out the best place to dive and where they could have sunfish nip at their toes. That was always a crowd pleaser.

Most summer people stayed only a week, and the Warrens were no exception. They said good-bye and took the train back to New York. The new guests who took their room did not want to drive in a hot car to swim in a cool lake, only to use the same hot car to come home and be just as hot as when they left. "What was the point?" they asked. So on such a lake-less afternoon I amused myself playing cowboys or Tarzan in the woods. But with Sonya still in the house, there were always endless hours of catch or just the two of us playing one-on-one baseball games that she always won. It was during one of those lopsided tilts that her mother came to us and announced that she knew where there was a wonderful patch of blueberries and she promised my mom she'd bring home enough for everyone's breakfast and cobblers, too. Sounded good to me. I was tired of having Sonya skunking me and proving she was more of a ballplayer than Joltin' Joe DiMaggio, Jackie Robinson and Ted Williams combined.

So my mother armed Mrs. Milligan with a large wicker basket lined with a soft towel and instructions to fill it to the top. She gave us kids two big coffee cans and the same orders. And so it was the three of us set out down the washboard dirt road that led past the house, not unlike Dorothy and her mates trudging off to find the Emerald City of Oz. Even Rover tagged along in the role of Toto. Mrs. Milligan said she discovered the nirvana of all blueberry patches on a trail off the Wild Acres Road about a mile away. That's a pretty rugged patch of woods, I remember thinking. We could run into bears. Little did I know the only things bare in those woods would be us.

I'm sure my mother preferred that I look like this rather than all covered with poison ivy after romping in the buff with two sun worshipers.

Sonya and I led the way, throwing stones into the brook, and before long Mrs. Milligan pointed to a rough opening in the thick underbrush. "All right, children, in you go," she said with her Austrian accent. The idea that the witch in Hansel and Gretel said the same thing darted briefly through my mind. No matter. Not more than fifty feet into the woods was a clearing surrounded by knee-high blueberry bushes heavy with fruit.

Mrs. Milligan put down the basket and proceeded to pick a plump berry and pop it into her mouth. She closed her eyes and said softly, "Delicious."

From under the towel in the basket she produced a bottle of Coppertone suntan oil. "Sonya, you need some sun," she announced and filled up her cupped hand with amber liquid. Sonya quickly removed her t-shirt and shorts and stood before her mother like a newborn fawn, all gangly arms and legs. Mrs. Milligan slathered the lotion all over Sonya's lean body and then looked at me. "Clifford, you need the sun, too."

I stood there, frozen, not quite sure what to do. "Come

on, take off your shirt and pants. Your mother wouldn't want you to get burned." No, I'm sure Mom wouldn't want me to get burned, but how would she feel about my getting undressed like this? Out in the woods. With two strange females. It was a question I didn't have to ponder long. Sonya pulled off my shirt and I kicked off my shorts and undies. I don't remember being embarrassed. I think it was more a feeling of uncertainty, not sure what to do next or what to expect. Outside of having my mom or Oma give me a bath on a Saturday night, I don't think I ever undressed in front of anyone before.

I turned my back to Mrs. Milligan and she doused my shoulders and arms with the stuff that smelled like coconuts. She handed me the bottle with instructions to put more on my front and before I could obey, Mrs. Milligan proceed to remove her clothes, too. Yikes. There we were, wearing nothing but Coppertone and smiles. Sonya took the bottle from me and proceeded to rub her mother's back and arms. "Play in the sunshine," Mrs. Milligan said lightly as she lay back on the grass and closed her eyes.

This play in the sunshine business was not new to me. As I served highballs during the after-dinner card games, Mrs. Milligan would freely tell everyone her religious philosophy about worshiping God outdoors. No cathedrals, chapels or churches for her. To get in touch with God, one just had to commune with nature, she advised. "That's an easy way to skip the collection plate," the old man once said and everyone laughed heartily. I wondered if they would be laughing now if they saw the three of us "communing with nature."

Sonya and I started to pick berries and I couldn't help noticing that while part of her body looked like mine, the other part didn't. "What are you looking at?" she said with a smirk as she punched me in the arm. "Don't you know nothing yet?" Apparently I didn't, and I looked down at the cluster of berries in front of me. Wow, I'd never forget this day. First, I find this massive blueberry patch and now I find that girls, even if they're tomboys, are different. Holy cow. Then there was Mrs. Milligan. Double holy cow.

After a while, Sonya lay down next to her mother, who by now had turned over on her stomach and was asleep. Maybe this is the way Tarzan really lives, I thought. Gee, no wonder he likes the jungle so much.

There's one thing to be said about picking blueberries naked: the branches can be rough on the hide. The Coppertone might be keeping me from burning, but it did nothing to keep the twigs and leaves from scratching. Then there were some pesky deer flies, too. They had a bite that left a good size welt and they seemed to like me as much as I liked the berries.

Sonya reached down and picked up a clod of dirt. She spit on it and rubbed the muddy mix on the bites on my back and shoulders. "Indians always do this," she said with some authority. I couldn't help wondering if this is something Roy Rogers and Dale Evans did when they were out on the trail. Nah. Roy would never take off one of those eagle-bedecked, long-fringed shirts he always wore.

Eventually Mrs. Milligan woke up from her nap and shaded her eyes as she squinted at the sun. She looked into our half-full coffee cans. "We'd better pick more if we want to be back in time for supper," she said kneeling down next to a clump of bushes. Sonya and I waded deeper into the thicket and I almost forgot that I didn't have anything on as I ate two or three berries for every five or six I put into the can.

After a while the can was full and so was I. "Let me see how much you have," Mrs. Milligan said as she motioned for us to join her. Smiling, she approved of our harvest. "Clifford, I know your mother will be pleased," she said. "We can cool off in the brook before going home." She picked up her clothes and made no effort to put them on. Sonya and I grabbed our stuff and followed her as she fearlessly made her way through the underbrush to the bank of the rapidly flowing brook. Leaving her basket of berries on some rocks she waded

Expenses

Paid Entered			
		Brought forward	10335?
June	—	mr White chairs & Table	9 00
"	29	C W Tuttle	3 00
"	"	— " —	1 7?
"	"	Chicken Feed	5 6?
"	"	Ice	5 ?
"	"	Dishes	2 00
"	"	Accident Ins on House @ 29.40 for 3 yrs.	9 80
"	"	Hotel Bus Ins.	4 60
"	"	1st Natl Stores	6 05
"	"	A.v.P.	2 44
July	6	1st Natl Stores	1 23
"	6	Tuttle	3 4?
"	"	Chicken Grain	5 08
"	6	Tuttle	4 90
"	"	— " —	1 6?
"	"	1st Natl	8?
"	6	A.v.P.	3 02
"	"	— " —	1 49
"	"	Tuttle	7 76
"	"	1st Natl	9 00
"	"	Bread & Chop meat	1 64
"	"	A.v.P.	1 76
"	"	Bond Bread	1 61
"	"	Ice	60
"	"	Eggs from Mrs Ernst	1 50
			1123 97

Dad kept accurate records of all expenses. From 1947, note the line items for hotel insurance – $4.60; and accident insurance – $29.40 for three years. Better to be covered lest one of the summer people twist a wrist while playing whist.

into the stream and eased herself into a deep pool of sparkling water. Sonya and I splashed in after her. We found flat stones and skipped them across the water to the far side and, in general, had kid fun in the cool water. There was something about not having anything on that was very refreshing. Mrs. Milligan closed her eyes, oblivious to our laughs and shouts, and floated in her private spa.

After some time she opened her eyes and squinted toward the sun, now slowly sinking behind the trees on the top of Mt. Pistareen. "All right, children, I think we should be going," she said as she climbed out of the water and stepped into her shorts that were laid out on the thick grass. Sonya gave me one last splash as she scrambled out of the brook and quickly got dressed. I followed but slipped on some mud and fell back into the water. Sonya extended her arm and as I grabbed it she jerked me out of the stream. "Come on, frog," she laughed as she tossed me into the weeds. I pulled on my shorts and shirt, snatched my bucket of berries and followed them toward the road.

We finally got home, just as mom and Oma started to get supper ready. They were busy and only gave perfunctory approval to my berry bounty and I had to quickly slip into my waiter outfit and set the tables. It wasn't until later that evening, as I was getting ready for bed, that I began to scratch and itch. Boy, did I scratch and itch. Mom only had to take one look at me, now covered with bumpy red patches, to know what the problem was. "Clifford, you're covered with poison ivy," she said with a shocked tone. "How did that happen? You know better than to touch poison ivy." That was true. But I couldn't exactly tell her it wasn't so much I touched the stuff, it's that it touched me, probably when Sonya pulled me from the brook and I rolled on the thicket of weeds without anything on. "How did you get it all over you?" Then she added with great motherly concern, "I hope we have enough calamine lotion."

As she went to retrieve the brown bottle with the pink liquid, I tried to resist the urge to scratch. But it was hard. I mean, I was one big itch and I rubbed my back against the bedpost to try and get some relief.

Mom was talking, half to me and half to herself, as she came back into the room carrying the bottle of calamine lotion and a box of cotton balls. "I don't see how you got it all over your back and legs, oh, and your chest, too," she said as she started to dab the cooling lotion on me. "Didn't Mrs. Milligan see the poison ivy and tell you to stay away from it? It's like you were running around naked."

Whoa, wait a minute. There was one of the words Charlie Warren used when he said he saw Mrs. Milligan that morning. Naked. Did it mean not having any clothes on? Hmmm, I wondered. "Like a nudist?" I asked.

She stopped dabbing and looked at me, a slight smile on her face. "Yes, like a nudist," she said with a hint of bemusement in her voice.

Wow, so that's what being a nudist meant. And now I am one, I thought. But something told me not to say, "Well, you see Mom, Mrs. Milligan was floating in the brook, naked, and Sonya was naked, too, when she pulled me, naked, out of the water so we all could get dressed and come home." No, I don't think that would have gone over too well.

"It's like you rolled in it," Mom said softly as she continued to dab me. When she was done, I looked like a stick covered with a hundred pink polka dots. Mom gave me clean pajamas and tucked me into bed with instructions not to scratch. From the screened porch someone called to her to come out, the pinochle game was about to begin. Phew, saved by a deck of cards.

That calamine was a miracle cure. The next morning I itched a lot less and another quick application insured that I would be scratch-free in a day or so. And Mom adjusted the sleeves on my waiter's jacket to make sure they covered the

23

calamine blotches on my arms, so no one would be grossed-out as they ate breakfast, highlighted with fresh blueberries. The berries were a big hit with everyone who had them on their cornflakes and in the pancakes I served.

At breakfast, Sonya and her mother sat at their table, but not one word was said about our adventure the day before. It was as if nothing unusual had happened. And maybe to them, nothing had. Perhaps Charlie Warren was right: Mrs. Milligan was a nudist, and so in her world, going around naked was just something she did. Like me wearing an oversized waiter's jacket, it was no big deal.

Two days later, Mrs. Milligan and Sonya went back to New York and wouldn't return until the next summer. Mom never asked how I managed to be covered with poison ivy. After all, everyone knew it was a part of living in the country. If you got into it, calamine lotion got rid of it. No big deal.

As for me, I never ran naked through the woods again. While it was fun, and I sure did learn a lot, being *au naturel* didn't seem natural. Besides, it resulted in too many questions with answers I don't think my family really wanted to hear.

AN OLD-FASHIONED
NEW ENGLAND THANKSGIVING

or

Never Get Run Over by a Headless Turkey

THERE'S ONE THING I have to say right off the bat; my old man never was very lucky when it came to winning things.

You've got to remember that the days of summer people were light-years before every state had a laundry list of lotteries with casinos and off-track betting parlors on every corner. Oh sure, if you lived in a big city you could see the guy who was the third cousin of your uncle's shop steward and he would take your bet on that hot tip you got from the kid at the gas station about the fifth race at Rockingham. But if that wasn't your cup of tea there always was the fabled Irish Sweepstakes with mystery horses racing a half a world away that held the excitement of fast money and the chance you would be forevermore identified as the lucky stiff who won the Irish Sweepstakes.

Our source for Irish Sweepstakes tickets was my mom's good friend, Joan Malloy, who lived in New York City. She was not an actual member of our family, but she was called Aunt Joan and was generous to a fault in every way it was possible to be generous. Birthdays, Christmas, Easter, and sometimes just when she saw something in a store on Fifth Avenue she thought we would like, a large bundle from New York would arrive at our post office and it would be Christmas Eve, regardless of the date on the calendar.

Aunt Joan was not only of Irish descent; she attended a Catholic church where Irish Sweepstakes tickets were apparently passed out as readily as wafers during communion. So she would buy a couple of tickets that, she assured us, had been blessed by the priest to bring extra good luck. However, some of the blessings must have worn off in the transit from Manhattan to Spofford, or else the Sweepstakes gods knew we were Lutherans attending a Methodist church and didn't think it was proper for non-papists to win the sacred pot of gold. But that curse didn't keep my father from sporadically buying a raffle ticket at a fireman's supper or the sheriff's annual summer fair. They never paid off but what the heck, he was only out a dime or a quarter. They never paid off, that is, except for one time.

It was early November 1948. The old man was working at the AO and, as he told the story, people were always selling raffle tickets for their kids' school or church bazaar. Sometimes he'd buy one but most of the time he passed. However, this one night a guy was selling tickets to win a live turkey just in time for Thanksgiving. There was one ticket left and the man said, "Come on, Fred. It's the last ticket but I can feel it's the winner. What do you say?" Well, it was only twenty-five cents so Dad reached into his pants pocket and there it was, one quarter. He handed it over, took the ticket, put it where the coin was, and forgot about it.

A week later the guy came up to Dad and said, "Freddie, you won! You won the turkey. See, I told you it was a lucky ticket. The bird's in my truck, you can take him home tonight."

There's a saying that goes, "No good deed ever goes unpunished." Well, in this instance it could be changed to "No lucky occurrence ever happens without dire consequences." Or something like that.

To begin with, Dad didn't have a truck to transport said

Tom turkey home that night. Still, his '39 Chevy was blessed with a cavernous trunk and the cage holding the bird fit comfortably. That is, after the spare tire, jack, snow shovel, and toolbox were removed and stored in the back seat.

"Won't he suffocate back there?" he asked as the cage was stuffed into the trunk. "Don't worry, Freddie, he'll be fine," he was told by the guy who sold him the winning ticket. "Nothing can kill these old birds." That was a line that would echo well past that Thanksgiving.

The first I learned about our good fortune was over breakfast the next morning. When he arrived home, the old man had wrestled the cage into the game room where he set up my baby crib, and used it to hold the bird.

Now, just so you know, the game room was next to the barn that served as our garage. It was a large space with a ping-pong table, upright piano, dart board, card table, and wicker settee where the summer people could go on a rainy day and amuse themselves until it was time for cocktails, which could occur at any moment of the day or night.

The game room was unheated and when I saw the big bird that cold November morning, I asked if he would freeze. "Don't worry," Dad said, "nothing can kill these old birds."

For the next two weeks I brought our feathery guest stale bread, cracked corn and water. My mom and Oma kept changing the newspapers on the floor of the crib and, from my way of thinking, that turkey had it as good as any of the summer people we served, except for the cocktails.

More importantly, Mom made calls to the New York relatives and invited them to partake in our good fortune and spend a real, old-fashioned New England Thanksgiving with us. "It will be perfect," she assured them.

It would also be a double celebration because Thanksgiving Day, November 25, was my parents' twelfth wedding anniversary.

But I had my own special reason to welcome this

Thanksgiving. It would be the first time I picked up a freshly severed turkey head.

Now wait, before you get your BVDs in a bunch, let me explain. As I have noted, we raised chickens for eggs but they were also a source of Sunday dinner. In order for that dinner to happen, something had to go; mainly the head of a chicken.

One of the many things my father had to learn when he abandoned city life and embraced a rural existence was how to dispatch a hen with one swing of the ax. It wasn't pretty but it had to be done. And he always did it behind the henhouse, out of sight of the summer people and the other chickens. But it didn't escape my hawk-eyed gaze. I always tagged after my father, even when he told me to stay in the garage while he walked to the chicken coop with an ax in his hand, because I had to see what was going on.

The old man and I might have looked innocent, but we struck fear in the hearts of chickens everywhere.

I peeked around the corner and saw him grab a chicken and, in one swift movement, he had the bird's neck splayed on a tree stump and he swung the ax. Ouch.

Looking up, he saw me and, rather than try and hide anything, calmly said, "Well, if you're going to look, you might as well see everything." He gestured to me to come forward and I did. "This is how we get that nice chicken dinner Oma cooks for us. Do you understand?"

I stared at the headless, flopping Barred Rock hen he held by the legs, blood dripping and staining the brown ground. I nodded slightly and saw the head lying at the base of the stump. For a long moment he didn't say anything. Then he turned and walked toward the house, "If you want to help, pick that up and we'll bury it." I picked it up by the red comb and looked at the slack beak. Did you know chickens have small feathers on their eyelids? "Don't look at it, just bring it along," he said without even turning back to see what I was doing.

And that was my introduction to becoming the best severed-chicken-head collector in all of New Hampshire. From that day forward, whenever Oma said chicken would be on the menu, Dad and I would walk down the hill to the chicken house and in a moment or two, he had the hens and I had the heads. We were an unbeatable team.

So when it became clear that a real live turkey was going to grace our table that Thanksgiving, my only thoughts were not about drumsticks, stuffing or even the wishbone. No, I was wondering if turkeys had pinfeathers on their eyelids, too.

While my father had become quite the dispatcher of chickens, and once even delivered the coup de grâce to a duck, this would be his first turkey. And it wasn't an ordinary turkey. This baby was twenty-five pounds or even more, thanks to all the bread and corn I was giving him. So the old man did what any professional would do; he asked for advice.

John Orr, the father of my best friend and our neighbor up the road, knew just about everything there was to know about anything, and he advised binding the big bird's wings with lots of strong twine. "He'll explode on ya," John said, "I've seen it happen. Those wings will knock ya to the ground if you ain't careful."

Wow, the thought of an exploding turkey rocked my six-year-old mind.

After conferring with my mother, Dad set the date of the turkey's demise. Because Mom and Oma would have to pluck and dress the giant fowl, which was not an easy feat, the most opportune time was deemed as early morning, Wednesday, November 24.

The relatives were notified. They were instructed to arrive Tuesday the 23rd and settle in for a long, relaxing Thanksgiving weekend.

It should be noted that travel from New York to New Hampshire in 1948 was slow and arduous at best. It was long before the Interstate highway system would crisscross the country, so the only way to get from here to there, or there to here, was via train or two-lane roads that seemed to wander through every town on the map. But who could refuse an invitation for a real, old-fashioned Thanksgiving dinner in the country? No one, that's who. And so they came. There was Oma's cousin, Marie, and her husband, Conrad Vogel, and their son, Walter, and his wife, Marge, and their two children, Walter and Marge. They all traveled in Walter's big Mercury. Next were Walter's sister, Martha, and her husband, Al, who were my godparents and finally, Aunt Joan, who took the train from Grand Central Station in New York to join the festivities. A good time was going to be had by all.

And so the day of reckoning was at hand, or neck or whatever. Tom turkey was about to meet his destiny: giblet gravy.

Early that morning, the old man and I went to the game room. Everyone was having breakfast, and the turkey must have been looking for his breakfast, too, because he was calmly clucking to himself as we entered the room. I watched silently as my father pulled out a ball of butcher's twine and moved the bird in to a corner of the crib and started to wrap the white cord around its wings. Now he was beginning to become nervous – the bird, not my father. Three, four, five times the cord went about the wings and breast of the bird who looked at both of us with eyes full of suspicion.

"All right, we're going to get the turkey ready for

tomorrow," the old man announced to the toast-munching, coffee-sipping multitude in the kitchen. "If you want to join us, we'll be at the henhouse in half an hour," he said as my mother handed him a cup of her strongest coffee.

Looking back on it now, that morning was misty and cold with the temperature in the upper 20s, not unusual for New Hampshire at that time of year. The bulk of the witnesses donned their heavy coats and hats and slowly made their way out of the house and down the lawn toward the henhouse. Little Walter and Marge, who were my age, were told to stay inside. The sight of a turkey being dispatched was thought to be too traumatic for them. Ha! Welcome to the country, cousins, where life is tough and only the scenery is pretty. City kids.

Mom and her best friend, Joan Malloy, a source of all things good, from Irish Sweepstakes tickets to healing potions, balms, salves, and very cool Christmas gifts.

Because the winters were so cold, we never tried to keep chickens during this time of the year, so the henhouse was empty and quiet. I took my place near the execution stump as the old man slowly made his way down the hill with an ax in his right hand and the bound turkey under his left arm. I say under his arm, but trying to put anything that weighs 25 pounds under your arm is not easy, especially when that 25 pounds is moving around, eyeing the ax and trying to escape.

Looking over my shoulder I saw the relatives standing at the crest of the hill, little puffs of steam coming from their noses. For an instant they reminded me of the black-and-white images I saw in the *Fox Movietone News* of the People's Politburo who stood above the Kremlin crowds and looked down on the pitiful Soviet citizens with disdain in their eyes as endless lines of troops and tanks rolled by.

Approaching the stump, the old man leaned slightly forward to extend the turkey's neck. And then it was done. Like Joe DiMaggio reaching out with his bat to slash a triple to the deepest corner of Yankee Stadium, Dad swung the ax and, with a dull thud, the turkey's head was separated from its body.

And that's when all hell broke loose.

John Orr sure knew what he was talking about. The turkey indeed exploded with a force that surprised the old man. Despite all the twine, the wings broke free and in a nanosecond, a headless, blood-spurting turkey was flying straight up in the air and then towards me.

For an instant I was frozen. There on the ground was my goal, my quest, my first turkey head. But there was also something I never counted on: a headless turkey coming directly at me.

All right, I'll admit it. I made a rookie mistake. I should have moved to either my left or my right, or just ducked, and let the headless creature pass by. But no, I turned and tried to run. Bad move. The frost made the ground hard and, in turning, I tripped over my feet. Down I went like a sack of freshly harvested potatoes and that headless turkey ran right over my back and landed in front of my face, fluttering with its last bit of life.

The Soviets on the hill watched without saying a word. I was so humiliated. My one big chance to score a turkey head and I blew it. Mom and Dad came to my rescue and helped me get up. "Go blow your nose," she directed as he hoisted the now-still bird by its feet and said softly, "That guy was right. Nothing can kill these old birds."

The next day the aroma of roasting turkey permeated the entire house for hours. In the kitchen the women prepared all sorts of wonderful things while the men sat around the fireplace smoking and drinking cocktails. At three in the afternoon, Oma and Mom served a golden brown turkey on a huge platter. The oohs and aahs must have been heard for miles around. Champagne was poured; toasts were made for the anniversary couple, and everyone was thankful for the abundance before us.

I, however, did not have any of the turkey that year. A little stuffing, a few Brussels sprouts and a dab of cranberry sauce was all I could manage to eat. To add insult to injury, I never had another opportunity to police the henhouse for a turkey head: the next Thanksgiving was our turn to visit the relatives in New York. It would be many years before the old man bought another raffle ticket for anything, and future Thanksgiving turkeys were supplied by the A & P with the word "Butterball" on them.

But it was just as well. I realize now that having a line on my résumé stating I was adept at collecting turkey heads would probably not have been a job enhancer.

JESUS WORE MY UNDERWEAR

or

The Catholics Clear Up a Lifetime of Confusion

RADIO HAS ALWAYS been a part of my life. Growing up in the wilds of New Hampshire, I had the radio as a constant companion day and night. It's not that we didn't know about television or fall under its hypnotic Cyclops eye, it's just that we lived in a valley surrounded by towering hills all but blocking even the strongest TV signal. In fact, when we finally got television, it was more of a challenge for the imagination than radio's theater of the mind. Peering at flickering black-and-white images and guessing – was that a man or a woman? Is that a dog or a horse? What's a dog doing in this scene anyway? It has to be a horse. Roy Rogers would never ride a dog. Yeah, it's a horse – it was hard to tell when everything was seen through a never-ending blizzard. Electronic snow was always six inches deep in our living room surrounding the 21-inch Sylvania.

So radio was the only option for tuning in to the world beyond our 57-acre wood in Spofford. Until 1958 there was only one local station; WKNE, 1290 on the AM dial broadcasting from Keene, New Hampshire.

It should be noted that back in the forties and fifties, saying AM was kind of redundant because FM was virtually unheard of, and besides, no one even had a radio that could pick up an FM signal. Yes sir, AM was all we

34

needed, thank you very much.

WKNE was a CBS affiliate, which meant we could hear news from around the world with Edward R. Murrow and his boys Charles Collingswood, Eric Sevareid, and a host of others. *The CBS World News Roundup* was there every morning at 8:00 with breaking news from far-flung hotspots around the globe: Berlin, Moscow, Paris, and London. The voices of despots and dictators, presidents and pipsqueak potentates came from the wooden cabinet of a little Emerson radio and flooded our kitchen. Then there was all the entertainment CBS offered: *Arthur Godfrey, The Adventures of Mr. and Mrs. North, Art Linkletter's House Party, Gunsmoke, Edgar Bergen and Charlie McCarthy, Jack Benny, Gene Autry's Melody Ranch, Our Miss Brooks, Lux Radio Theater* and my mother's favorite, *The Romance of Helen Trent.*

Mom insisted on total silence during lunch at 12:30 every afternoon as she listened to Helen's valiant quest to prove "that because a woman is 35, or older, romance in life need not be over... that the romance of youth can be extended into middle-life and even beyond..." She always managed to have that break no matter how busy the dining room. My father and I were glad Helen's crusade lasted only fifteen minutes a day. On the brighter side, after straightening up the rooms, Mom spent summer afternoons filled with the sounds of Red Sox baseball as Kurt Gowdy called the play-by-play and the Fenway faithful cheered in vain for the Sox to win a pennant. Any pennant.

But despite everything CBS supplied, it was WKNE's local announcers who intrigued me most. Every morning began with the deep baritone of Ozzie Wade, radio host extraordinaire. Ozzie was the quintessential "morning man." He made funny remarks, told corny jokes, played popular music, and would even stop a record he didn't like and smash it to make sure we listeners would never have to hear it again. He also drank coffee by the gallon, slurping it long and loud as he proclaimed, "Now that's a good cup of coffee! Joe at the Crystal Restaurant on the Square brought it in and he said to remind you they've got hot apple turnovers this morning. I've got one here in front of me, and when you dunk it in a cup of their fine coffee, you can't have a bad morning!"

Holy socks! Guys brought Ozzie Wade free food! No wonder he was so cocky and sure of himself. That's what must have inspired him to do the things he did. Sometimes he'd say, "Well, let's see what the bonehead network people in New York are talking about this morning," and he'd fade in CBS for a few seconds. "Boy, are we lucky we don't have to listen to that," he'd say as he started a wacky record by Spike Jones and the City Slickers. Oh, what power! What freedom! I wondered what it would be like to have such a life.

And then it happened. Poets might call it kismet but I choose to think of it as one of the best days of my life. It occurred while shopping with my parents at the A & P in Keene. As Bogey said in *Casablanca*, "It appears that destiny has taken a hand." Destiny, hah! This was more like total divine intervention. For that day, that seemingly uneventful day at the A & P, was to me akin to the day Einstein discovered relativity, or the day Ted Williams became the last baseball player to end the season with a batting average over .400, or the day Jack Benny found his first nickel on the street. That's because the guy in front of us at the checkout was none other than Ozzie Wade himself.

The clerk was joking with him and my mom turned to me and said in a whisper, "That's Ozzie Wade!"

Yikes! Ozzie Wade! My heart nearly exploded. It was like meeting Santa Claus, the Easter Bunny, and the Tooth Fairy all at once. I held my breath for a moment as I listened to him talk to the A & P guy. Yes, it really was Ozzie! There was no mistaking that coffee-slurping baritone voice.

"We listen to you every morning," Mom said with a smile as she turned so I could see the great man. "We live in Spofford and my son Clifford is your biggest fan." Ozzie chuckled and looked down at me.

It is only fair to point out that Ozzie Wade had what could be called a "face for radio." He was stocky, balding and wore thick glasses. What little hair he had was gray and plastered across the top of his head in a feeble attempt to make it look like he had more hair than he really did. Ozzie was not at all what I had seen in my mind's eye. But it didn't matter. He was talking to me.

"So Clifford, would you like to see the radio station?" he asked.

Oh, my God, not only was Ozzie Wade talking to me, he was willing to take me into the hallowed halls of WKNE, the one place on earth where everything was pure and decent and good. I don't remember answering; I just looked up at him, slack-jawed. While I meant it to be reverence, I realized later than my hero could easily have interpreted my stunned reaction as that of a half-wit.

"We'd love to see the radio station," my mom gushed.

"Good," Ozzie said as the clerk handed him a pack of Chesterfields and some change. "Come by in thirty minutes, if you can, and tell the receptionist you'd like a tour."

"Can we? Can we really go?" I asked, nearly peeing my pants just thinking about the opportunity. My mother looked at Dad and he smiled and nodded agreement.

YES! Not only had destiny taken a hand, she owned the whole deck.

Dad paid for our groceries and asked the clerk if he knew where the radio station was, and he gave us the directions.

Exactly thirty minutes later, we pulled into the gravel parking lot of WKNE. Inside, the receptionist said Ozzie was expecting us. And there he was, Ozzie the radio wizard, cracked coffee cup in hand, holding open the door to his kingdom, the inner sanctum of sound where all things were possible.

First he showed us the studio where he did his morning

show. It was cramped, jammed tight with three turntables and a control board full of knobs and dials and a large diamond-shaped microphone suspended from the ceiling by two small chains. My head spun. In the back of the studio was a floor-to-ceiling rack of records and more electronics that Ozzie said gave him remote readings from the transmitter.

I was caught up in the sights and the smells, the mingled scent of cigarettes, coffee, and warm electronic equipment. It was a heady perfume and as intoxicating as any cocktail concocted by the summer people.

He took us to the small newsroom where a Teletype machine chattered in the corner, spitting out an endless sheet of paper with news from around the state and the world.

Finally he led us into the studio where live programs were aired. I was most impressed by the walls. They were covered with white tile squares, with hundreds of holes in them. Ozzie explained that they were special acoustical tiles that gave the room the sound needed for broadcasting.

The old man glanced at his watch and said we had to go. Ozzie shook my hand and thanked me for coming. Not only had I met Ozzie Wade, he also showed me where he did his show and he shook my hand. I could die a happy kid.

On the way home, in the back seat of the Chevy, I had an epiphany. At that moment, in one brilliant, all-encompassing flash of light I knew what I wanted to do with my life. I would become a radio announcer just like Ozzie Wade! Yes, think of it. I could mock people in exotic places like New York, make rude sounds with any kind of beverage, and play funny music all day long. So long Roy Rogers. Goodbye Gene Autry. How stupid I'd been for wanting to ride the range like you saps and shoot bad guys. Hah! Every kid in my second grade class had that dream. Forget it. Being a cowboy was for losers. That was a sucker's job. I was about to answer a nobler calling. I would be a coffee-slurping, record-playing, wisecracking disc jockey. I would be someone my family could be proud of as they turned on the radio and proclaimed to the world, "That's our boy!"

With my career path chosen, I began to listen even more intently to everything broadcast on WKNE. Even that odd fifteen minutes between 7:45 and 8.00 every Saturday morning when the *Rosary* was on.

Now, the only church in Spofford was United Methodist. We were Lutheran, as rare as palm trees in that part of New Hampshire, but we went to the local church where Mom and Dad taught Sunday school. Oddly enough, there was never any mention of a Rosary.

The first time I heard the repetitious chanting, I asked the old man what was going on and he explained that the Rosary was a Roman Catholic devotion consisting of meditation on sacred mysteries while saying Hail Marys. The explanation didn't make much sense, but I did know about Hail Marys. I had New York-based cousins who went to Catholic school and they told tales of terror inflicted on them whenever they did something that was perceived as bad. Whisper in class, whack, a nun would crack a wooden ruler across their knuckles. And to make things right, they had to say a bunch of Hail Marys. Anything could trigger this punishment, including eating a hot dog on Friday. I was glad the Methodists were more open-minded about menu choices.

So I didn't pay much attention to the Saturday *Rosary* broadcast. After all, it was only fifteen minutes of precious airtime, and usually we would just turn the volume down and not pay any attention to what was going on. That is, until one Saturday. I was still in bed, praying to my Lutheran/Methodist God to get the Catholics off the air so Ozzie Wade could come up with another cool way to make obnoxious sounds with his coffee. My mind raced at the prospects. Perhaps Ozzie would include forcing it out of his nose the way I'd seen Sonya Milligan do when she grossed out everyone in the dining room.

Suddenly something in the Rosary hit me. It wasn't the "Hail Mary, full of grace, the Lord is with thee, blessed art thou amongst women," part. We Lutheran/Methodists knew all about Mary and how she was chosen by God to give birth to Jesus. It was the next line... "And blessed is the Fruit of the Loom, Jesus."

At first I thought I must have been dreaming. Did those Catholics really say, "Blessed is the Fruit of the Loom, Jesus"? I tried to filter out the small talk from my mom and dad in the next room.

"Hail Mary, full of grace, the Lord is with thee, blessed art thou amongst women, and blessed is the Fruit of the Loom, Jesus." They said it again! Fruit of the Loom, Jesus. Could it be? The savior of mankind, the Son of God, the real reason we celebrate Christmas, Jesus the Christ wore the same kind of underwear as me?

We'll probably never know if Roy Rogers wore Fruit of the Loom underwear. But this cowboy did, and he always pondered the nagging question: Was Jesus a Fruit of the Loom man?

Scrambling out of bed, I pulled open the underwear drawer in my bureau. Sure enough, there they were, labels at the back of each pair of underpants and shirts. Bunches of ripe fruit and the words, Fruit of the Loom. This was amazing! How come the Lutheran/Methodists never mentioned this? Was it something the Catholics just discovered? Did their New Testament begin, Matthew, Mark, Luke, John, and the Clothing Catalogue According to the Messiah?

I didn't dare say anything to anyone about this, but the

following Saturday morning I turned the radio up at 7:45. "Blessed is the Fruit of the Loom, Jesus." There it was. Again and again. "Turn down that damned *Rosary*," the old man yelled from the bedroom. I did, but just a little. I wanted to make sure, absolutely, positively sure, because this was something I was going to bring up in Sunday school the next day. Who knows, maybe my discovery would lead the lost to the Lord. Those who were nonbelievers, the unwashed heathens in our midst, might suddenly think, "Hey, this Jesus guy is okay. He wears Fruit of the Loom. I can relate to that. You think he drives a Chevy, too?"

But my chance never came. That old destiny thing reared her tousled head again. The next day I had a cold and my mother didn't think I should infect the other Sunday school kids, so I stayed home. "Maybe it's better this way," I thought. "Maybe I shouldn't say anything about the Catholics and their belief that Jesus wears Fruit of the Loom. After all, didn't my dad say the Rosary was a Catholic devotion consisting of meditation on sacred mysteries? Yeah, he did say that. And maybe one of those mysteries was how Jesus wore Fruit of the Loom 2,000 years ago. But he only shared that wisdom with the Catholics." So I decided to just shut up and keep this divine manifestation to myself. Besides, if the Lutheran/Methodists started believing what Catholics believed, maybe we'd have to give up hot dogs on Fridays. Yeah. Better not tell this to anyone. It will just be a little secret between Jesus and me.

NEARLY FIFTEEN YEARS later, when my dream of being a disc jockey had become a reality, I was working at a radio station in Albany, New York. My program was on from 8:00 to 11:00 every night. However, 7:00 to 8 o'clock was an hour of news and religious programs, and one of them was the *Rosary*.

I really didn't give it much thought. There were several *Rosary* flavors including sorrowful, joyful, glorious, and luminous. The program log indicated which one to play, I read

41

the introduction script, started the tape and turned the speakers down as I gathered up records for my show.

But one night I heard something that rang the proverbial bell. "Blessed is the Fruit of the Loom, Jesus." That phrase. Where had I heard that phrase before? Suddenly the image of Christ in underwear came flooding back. I put on my headphones and turned up the volume, anxious to catch every word. This might be the vindication I'd been seeking for all these years. And there it was... "Blessed is the fruit of thy womb, Jesus."

Thy womb! All this time they were saying, "thy womb"? No wonder I didn't get it when I was six. I had no idea what a womb was. So those Catholics didn't have any secret enlightenment and they weren't on to something profound and revealing. Jesus wasn't wearing my underwear after all. Catholic children were just like the rest of us, except they couldn't eat hot dogs on Friday and got their knuckles smashed if they did.

Wow. "Good thing I didn't tell those Sunday school kids my discovery," I thought. They would have laughed me out of the class; although, if one of them had snorted milk out of his nose during snack time, it would have been worth it. I know Ozzie Wade would have been proud.

THE FACTS OF LIFE

or

Episcopal Priests Don't Know Much About the Birds and Bees

SEX. THAT LITTLE THREE-LETTER WORD that is so full of dynamite. Or TNT, to employ three equally explosive letters. Stroll through the checkout aisle of any grocery store and you are bombarded with magazine covers apoplectic about sex.

"INCREASE YOUR SEX LIFE BY 100%!"

"SEX SECRETS THAT WILL DRIVE HIM WILD!"

"LOOK SEXIER – LOSE 10 POUNDS IN 10 DAYS!"

"LOSE 10 POUNDS IN 10 DAYS WITH SEX SECRETS THAT WILL DRIVE HIM 100% WILD!"

Well, you get the idea. And the electronic media, radio, and television, not to mention the Internet, are equally obsessed with the subject. The old advertising dictum that sex sells has never been truer. It is as if sex has a limited shelf life and if you don't get in on it right now, it will be gone and you will be tough out of luck.

I know, sex is how we all got here and the desire for it is just a part of Mother Nature's wacky little plan to make sure everything – from amoebas to humans – stick around. Fine. Live with it. However, the barefaced hawking of sex has never been more in your face and will undoubtedly become even more strident, if that's possible, in the future.

It is no wonder parents are concerned about this

43

type of exposure to their children. Many stores actually are aware of this and offer a few checkout aisles that are not lined with magazines so mom and her little tykes don't have to run the gauntlet of sleaze and depravity while paying for the Cocoa Puffs.

But during the time of the summer people, things were less sexually frenetic. That's not to say sexual things weren't lurking around the corner or on the edges of the night or the woods. That naked romp with Mrs. Milligan and Sonya was eye opening and the traveling salesman/farmer's daughter jokes that were casually told over the canasta games always resulted in lecherous laughter that I suspected was something only for adults to understand.

That said, one of the summer people once left a 3-D movie magazine with a picture of Marilyn Monroe in it that, when you wore those special glasses, exploded off the page and allowed Marilyn's bountiful charms to tumble into your hands. Wowzer.

And naturally, whenever something is restricted or banned, it becomes even more enticing. That's the way it was with the movie, *The Moon Is Blue*. It came out about the same time Marilyn was coming out of the fan magazine, and it was condemned by the Catholic Church's League of Decency, which resulted in it being banned in Boston. The double-whammy. Not being Catholic, I wasn't aware of the League, but my papist friend, Frankie Clooney, filled me in on everything. He said the priests in his church condemned the film and anyone who saw it would take the direct train to Hell. Not the local with stops in Purgatory, no, this was the high-ballin' express to Beelzebub's front door. "Geez, it must have something very bad in it," I said to him. He agreed. "I wonder how we can see it," I added. But Frankie's eyes got really big, and he backed away from me as if I were handing out first-class tickets on the Hell Limited. "Not me," he said as he turned away, "It's bad enough when you eat a hot dog on Friday. Count me out."

It was probably the curse that affects all youth: the feeling of invincibility and thinking nothing bad can happen to them. After all, what if Frankie was right and just seeing a movie like that could buy a kid a one-way ticket to Satan's sauna? But what if the ticket was free and no actual money was spent on the sin? Hmm.

Frankie's father, Sean, worked in the distribution office of Paramount Pictures in New York and got passes to theaters all around the country. When he and his family became summer people, he would occasionally hand out passes to theaters in Keene or Brattleboro. I was very impressed with that. Even though kid tickets were usually no more than twenty-five cents, it was hip to hand the ticket-taker a pass while all the other schlubs were standing in line to buy their tickets. Besides, that quarter would come in handy for movie junk food.

As luck would have it I had some passes stashed away for just such an occasion. Excellent. Now I just needed a theater showing *The Moon Is Blue* and someone to share the thrill of being bold and bad. Obviously, it had to be someone who wasn't Catholic. And then it hit me. Of course – my friend Johnny Orr who just lived up the road and played cowboys with me all the time. He also attended the Methodist church and so was exempt from Catholic guilt and the damnation that went with it.

So the next time Johnny and I rode the imaginary range together, I told him about the movie and how we had to see it. He wasn't as enthusiastic as I hoped he would be, and wanted to know if there was a chance cowboys might be in it. I said I doubted the Catholic Church would condemn a cowboy movie. "It must have something like Marilyn Monroe in 3-D in it," I argued. That concept got his attention and he agreed to go with me.

A few weeks after our plan to see the condemned film was conceived, I was in Keene shopping with my parents when I walked past the Colonial Theater and saw a poster that said,

"Coming Soon, *The Moon Is Blue*. Banned in Boston but not in Keene!"

Who knew Keene was such a wide-open town? I couldn't wait to tell Johnny. Our patience paid off and the next week the Colonial had on its marquee, "Now Showing – *The Moon Is Blue*."

The trip to Keene would require some delicate maneuvering. My parents always shopped in the morning and matinees never started before 2:00 PM so going with them and getting lost for a few hours was out of the question. Besides, I had tables to serve and bus. However, Johnny's mom liked to have her hair done in Keene and we knew that took several hours which would give us enough time to become men of the world.

If you were a ticket seller and these two tried to pass themselves off as being 18 years old, would you believe them? Fat chance.

So two days later, Johnny came running down the road and said his mom was going to the beauty parlor the next afternoon and we could ride in with her. I asked Mom if I could go and she agreed – providing I had all my chores done. I practically rushed everyone through lunch that day so I'd be ready to satisfy my youthful prurient interests.

As soon as Mrs. Orr parked the car and stepped into the salon, we headed straight for the Colonial. The sense of forbidden adventure stirred in my blood and I knew I was on the verge of satisfying some primal instinct I didn't quite understand.

As we approached the ticket booth a big sign stopped us in our tracks. "No one under 18 admitted." Eighteen? I had just turned 11 and Johnny was only a few months older. Life could be so cruel. Quickly we agreed it was worth the chance to see if we could talk our way past the lady in the booth. Because Johnny was actually older, I gave him the passes and he strode up to the ticket booth and in his deepest voice asked for two tickets as he slid them across the marble counter.

The ticket lady looked at us and asked the fateful question, "You boys eighteen?"

"Almost," Johnny answered.

She shook her head. "Gotta be eighteen. Sorry."

I hadn't come this far to let a ticket seller turn me away, and I stepped next to Johnny. "My friend's father works for the movie company and he gave us the passes so we could see it."

Her eyes narrowed as she took a hard look at us. Let me tell you, there is nothing tougher than a recalcitrant New England movie ticket seller.

"Eighteen," she said firmly and pushed the passes back.

Our childish response was to turn tail and run down the street. The frustration of not knowing why the Catholic bishops put the kibosh on this movie was maddening, but we had been shot down, shut out, and there was nothing we could do about it.

As it turned out, our prepubescent yearning for carnal knowledge would have led to even more frustrations if we had gotten in to see the film. While hoping to see someone like movie-magazine Marilyn, I eventually learned *The Moon Is Blue* was considered offensive only because its actors uttered the words, "virgin", "seduce" and "mistress." Boy, am I glad we didn't waste good passes just for a cheesy vocabulary lesson.

So the rest of that summer and for the whole next year,

3-D glasses and fan magazines satisfied the desire to sample forbidden fruit.

Sadly, 3-D magazines featuring voluptuous movie stars turned out to be a fad that seemingly disappeared forever. As far as I was concerned, they were one of the greatest marvels of the 20th century and I could never understand their demise. Perhaps those rascally Catholic bishops had something to do with it.

IN THE MEANTIME, while I was becoming emotionally involved with Marilyn's extra-dimensional charms in print, Mom read and relied on her favorite magazine, the *Ladies' Home Journal*, for advice on just about everything. Dedicated to celebrating motherhood, it showed how moms like mine could protect the future of American democracy through the performance of selfless, hands-on mothering. Who could argue with that? Toss in a couple of good meatloaf and pineapple-upside-down-cake recipes and it's no wonder moms everywhere eagerly awaited the latest issue.

Part of all that maternal material touched on the trials and tribulations of teaching children about life, specifically the facts of life. That is to say, sex.

One of the other magazines we received regularly was *The Saturday Evening Post*, which, in the 1950s, more often than not featured a cover depicting a slice of American life as interpreted by Norman Rockwell. One issue in particular made an impact on my impressionable mind and that was a cover called, "The Facts of Life." It was on the July 14, 1951, issue and showed a typical father of that era, complete with white shirt and bow tie, seriously talking to a boy who is obviously his son. Across the dad's knee is an open book entitled *The Facts of Life*. The boy appears to be about 12 or 13, his chin is in his hands, he's blushing and has a look of dread on his face as he listens to what his dad is telling him. As a kid, I usually understood *Post* covers and even found most of them amusing. But this one perplexed me and I admit I didn't get it. Not then, anyway. But I would several years later when it became my time to get the talk. Or lecture. Or lesson. Or whatever it was.

Here's where the *Ladies' Home Journal* comes in. I always looked at the *Post* because it had great cartoons that I would clip and put in a scrapbook. The *Journal* didn't have much humor so I didn't pay much attention to it. But one day, I passed the dining room table where there was a copy open to a page that talked about adolescents and the facts of life. There was even a coupon to send away for a book that explained everything.

Hmm. Suddenly that Norman Rockwell cover came back to mind. Was the old man going to make me go through what the kid in the picture was experiencing? I had already heard enough lectures in my young life, and I didn't need one more. Besides, if this facts of life stuff was what I thought it was, I could probably tell him a thing or two. Well, in general terms anyway. See, I was a Boy Scout and had attended several Jamborees with older kids who talked and bragged endlessly about girls and their adventures together. It was stuff never covered in the Boy Scout handbook. At first I didn't know what these guys were talking about, but I soon learned it was better to laugh along with them than to ask questions. Question-askers were labeled "babies" – or worse. No sir, not me. I just took it all in and considered this knowledge as one step on the way to making me a man of the world.

Several days later, Mom asked me to take a handful of letters to the post office, and I noticed that the one at the top of the stack was addressed to the *Ladies' Home Journal* someplace in Iowa. Yikes, my mother was sending away for the book and that meant the talk was coming.

Before continuing, I want to say one thing about the *Ladies' Home Journal*. While my mom might have clung to its every word to make her a better mother, this magazine was not without its missteps. For instance, in December of 1900 the *Journal* made a list of predictions for the coming one hundred years – and some of them were doozies. For instance, Nicaragua would ask for admission to the United States, and Mexico would do the same followed by many other South and Central American countries. And how about this one: There will be air-ships, but they will not successfully compete with surface cars and water vessels for passenger or freight traffic. They will be maintained as deadly war-vessels by all military nations. The *Journal* also predicted that city traffic would be either underground in subways or above ground on tall train trestles, insuring that all cities would be free from noise. And my personal favorite was that there would be no C, X or Q in our everyday alphabet. Those letters would be abandoned because they were unnecessary. Gadzooks, that would squelch my first name as well as the word "squelch." I wondered if my mom knew about these loony predictions and, if she did, how that would affect her opinion of the *Journal* and the advice it offered.

But it was too late. She sent away for the facts of life book and in a few weeks it arrived. There it was, in a brown envelope with her name on it and the *Journal*'s return address. "It won't be long now," I thought.

Don't get me wrong; it wasn't that I didn't want to get the facts of life, but what I already knew made discussing the subject with my parents very uncomfortable. And maybe that was one of life's facts.

For some unknown reason, Mom stashed the booklet from the *Journal* in the top drawer of a bureau in the dining room. This large piece of furniture held table linens, candlesticks and holders and tons of other household items. I was looking for a set of colored pencils for a school project when I found it. The title was pretty straightforward and centered on talking to your child about sex.

Naturally, I was intrigued and, glancing over my shoulder

to make sure no one was around, I started to read it. It even had line drawings to help the narrative along and it certainly filled in the gaps between the Boy Scout stories and the traveling salesman jokes the summer people told. Suddenly, I had a clearer picture of what all these facts were about and why a parent might be embarrassed talking about them. Putting the booklet back exactly where I found it, I didn't dare let on about my discovery.

Dad always drove me to the bus stop on school days, and we usually talked about baseball or a movie I wanted to see. But one day, he came right out and asked if I knew anything about the facts of life. "You mean where babies come from and junk like that?" I answered. Yes, that's what he meant. "Sure, I know all about that from school," I said rather offhandedly. He didn't say anything else except good-bye as I got out of the car. Whew. I wondered if he was as relieved as I was that we both dodged that bullet.

School ended that year, the summer people returned and so did my table-waiting duties. Our closest neighbor was St. Anne's Camp for girls, run by the Sisters of St. Anne, an Episcopal order of nuns. It was open from mid-June to the end of August, and many parents who came to visit their camper daughters stayed at The Maples.

Because nuns ran the camp, a priest had to be in residence to conduct the services of the Episcopal High Church. There was also an Episcopal Low Church, but the St. Anne's nuns would rather skip a service if it meant lowering themselves to go to a Low. We Lutheran/Methodists always thought it peculiar, but never questioned their allegiance to the High and the Almighty.

While the old man never mentioned the facts of life again, Mom apparently thought the subject wasn't finished yet. After all, she had that booklet from the *Journal* and its contents hadn't been discussed. So she pressed one of the summer people into performing the deed.

Father Charles Conklin was the St. Anne's priest that summer. After conducting his daily clerical duties, he enjoyed spending the evening on our screened porch with a cocktail or two.

Episcopal priests can marry, but Father Conklin admitted he was not the marrying kind. Dad cynically observed that he thought Conklin's favorite color was lavender, "If you get my drift," he added, evasively.

Nonetheless, Mom recruited Father Conklin to broach the subject of love, life, and lust with me. His approach was not without its humor, although I suspect very unintentional.

We had no other houseguests that particular week and I was reading a comic book on the porch when the good Father sat next to me and asked if I enjoyed seeing all the beautiful girls at the camp. I thought it an odd question for a man of the cloth to ask and shrugged, "I guess so." He blithely went on to point out that many of them were developing into young women as their bodies changed and he asked if I knew why it was happening.

At this point he was starting to sound creepy and I got up to leave but he grabbed my arm and said, "Clifford, there are things you must know about women. Take me to your record player, I have something I want you to listen to," and he pulled a record from his jacket pocket.

Now things were really getting strange, but I was sort of interested in hearing the record. I led him to the portable hi-fi we had in an alcove off the dining room and he put on the disc. Out of the speakers came Frank Sinatra singing, "Blues in the Night."

> "My mama done tol' me, when I was in knee-pants
> "My mama done tol' me, Son, a woman'll sweet talk
> "And give ya the big eye, but when the sweet talkin's done
> "A woman's a two-face, a worrisome thing
> who'll leave ya to sing the blues in... the night.

I couldn't believe what I was hearing and I wasn't referring to Frank. No, I meant the song, and I was confused about the message. By now "Ol' Blue Eyes" was in full-throated action, going,

> *"...the rain's a-fallin', hear the train a-callin', 'Whooee!'*
> *"My mama done tol' me.*
> *Hear that lonesome whistle blowin' 'cross the trestle,*
> *'Whooee!'"*

What the heck did a train on a trestle have to do with girls' bodies turning into women? Wait a minute. That *Ladies' Home Journal* prediction for the year 2000 said trains would travel over cities on tall trestles. Is that what this is all about? I was beginning to feel like the kid in the Rockwell painting, only worse.

> *"My mama done tol' me.*
> *A-whooee-dah-whooee, o' clickety-clack's a-echoin' back*
> *the blues in the night..."*

"Listen closely," Father Conklin said, "It is time you learn all women will have you singing the blues in the night."

Huh? Is that the ultimate fact of life: some babe will turn me into a nightclub singer? I didn't even like Frank Sinatra. How come the Boy Scouts never mentioned Frank when they were talking about rolling around in the back of their cars with their girlfriends? Was this the real message my momma wanted to tell me? My head was swimming.

"I-I-I know all about that stuff," I stammered, "Gotta go!" I pulled away and rushed to my room, still hearing the music playing when I closed the door. This guy was beyond weird. He was bizarre with a capital Z. If this guy represented the High Church, I shuddered to think what went on in the lowly Low version.

I had read that *Journal* booklet from cover to cover, and there was no mention of Frank Sinatra singing anything. I was going to have to bring this up at the next Jamboree. No, that probably wouldn't be wise. I decided to just keep my mouth shut and ears open. Those older scouts knew more about the facts of life than any Episcopal priest. Besides, I bet their taste in music leaned more to rock 'n' roll, and I was sure I could learn a lot from those lyrics. Just listen to "Work With Me, Annie" and you'll know what I mean.

THE BEDSHEET PARACHUTE

or

Jumping Off the Roof Was My Mom's Idea

THERE'S AN OLD ADAGE that goes like this: A little knowledge is a dangerous thing. How true. Not only is it dangerous, it can break your neck.

As a kid of 10, I don't think I knew the true meaning of "cabin fever," at least not the way adults appreciated that phrase. For the uninitiated, it refers to the crazy things people do to combat the result of being confined to a cabin, their home, for long periods during the winter. Grownups, I noticed, usually got twitchy toward the end of February, especially if it had been a very bad winter with snow up to the second-story windows and temperatures below zero for days on end. But even if it was a comparatively mild winter, the bleakness of February could cause a crack in the psyche of even the strongest among us. It's not unlike the dreaded solitary confinement in prison. Opponents of solitary confinement claim that it is a type of cruel and unusual punishment and a form of torture because of the sensory deprivation that often goes with it, all of which can have a severe negative impact on a person's mental state that can lead to depression or even death. Yikes. All that in the month that features Valentine's Day.

Combating cabin fever took many forms, not the least of which were imbibing too much alcohol, spending excessive amounts of time and money ordering things from the

Montgomery Ward catalog, and, for the truly fortunate, closing up their cabin and going to Florida for a few weeks. The weird thing was, one never knew when the fever would hit and how the victim would react and what odd behavior would result.

One notorious incident involved a Sunday school teacher at a nearby church who disappeared without a trace. Volunteers searched for her in the woods, in barns, in closed-up summer cottages. Everyone was frantic. Had she been abducted by a band of Gypsies? Did she decide to go ice fishing? Did she fall through the hole in the ice? Did a secret lover whisk her off to a romantic hideaway? Boy Scouts looked over hill and dale. Heck, they even looked over Roy and Dale without success. Finally, after a week she returned home. It seemed that being confined to her house with three children and a husband who had colds, the flu, chicken pox, and German measles all at once, caused her to snap. So she took off for Boston where she stayed at the YWCA, went shopping in Filene's Basement, saw foreign films in little movie theaters, and ate at a different Chinese restaurant every day. Her explanation was "cabin fever" that a good dose of Boston cured. No one questioned this explanation because they all knew as soon as the weather warmed and the snow retreated, all would be fine again. And it was.

What was unusual, however, was that a kid would be vexed with the curse of cabin fever. That was practically unheard of. After all, kids didn't have the concerns of the world weighing on their shoulders the way adults did. Oh sure, there was school with mind-numbing multiplication tables to memorize and the mental gymnastics needed to survive surprise spelling tests. (What's with that "i before e except after c" business? Or is it the other way around?) Of course, failure to excel at these scholastic exercises would result in report card grades that always raised parental eyebrows and more often than not resulted in denial of some privilege or amusement.

Hmm. Now that I think about it, maybe kids did have a susceptibility to cabin fever. Being told to go outside and play even in the coldest, snowiest weather always cured any behavior deemed out of the ordinary. But one well-thrown ice ball to the eye made the cabin look much more appealing, fever or not.

However, my touch of cabin fever didn't stem from a snowball fight or any other ice ball-induced incident. No, as far as I can backtrack, reading a science book generated it.

It was late February and I was in the fifth grade, taught by Mrs. Bromwell, a large, sagging woman who wore bedroom slippers because they were the only comfortable footwear she could find for her size-10 feet. She reminded me a lot of Eleanor Roosevelt, without the humor and sympathy factor. Anyway, we were studying Leonardo da Vinci's inventions and discoveries. Most of them I found tedious. Oh sure, his scheme for diverting the flow of the Arno River was probably all the rage of the day. But his musical instruments, hydraulic pumps, reversible crank mechanisms, and even a steam-powered cannon bored me. But then I turned a page in the book and saw something that stirred my imagination and banked the fires of cabin fever in my soul.

It was a sketch Leonardo made of a design for a modern parachute, and he did it back in 1483. Holy smoke, this guy was a genius after all. He was thinking about a parachute and didn't have an airplane to jump out of. I brought this up to Mrs. Bromwell who pointed out that the original idea was to use the parachute as a way to escape from tall buildings without injury.

Suddenly I saw old Leonardo in a whole new light. Parachuting from a plane was always a dream of mine, but it would probably mean I would have to join the Army, which was not very realistic at the age of 10. But Leo saw people jumping out of, or off of, buildings and as everyone knew, back in his day buildings weren't very tall, just like the one I lived in, so, i.e., *ergo*, I could put his plan in action right here at home.

That's it! I would use da Vinci's parachute to jump off the roof of our house!

I was dizzy with possibilities. Not only would I ace this science class, I would also put my knowledge to practical use and prove that a 470-year-old idea was accurate. My parents would raise their eyebrows in a good way and they would reward me with comic books and 3-D movies forever. I was also ready to collect my Nobel Peace Prize.

Studying the ancient da Vinci sketch was helpful but his dimensions were wacky. I mean, the old boy called for a length of gummed linen cloth with a length of 12 yards on each side and 12 yards high. The 12-times multiplication table that had been drummed into my head quickly came into play and I suddenly realized that all that memorization might have some value after all. Let's see, a yard is three feet and 12 yards would be...yikes, 36 feet. And the formula called for 36 feet of fabric on each side and in height. Impossible. Where was I going to get that much material? Besides, our house was only 55-feet high, which meant I'd be on the ground before my parachute opened and that would no way be a successful jump.

It was obvious I was going to have to make something of my own design. Sorry, Leo, it's back to history books for you, pal.

There's one thing about being shut up in a house during the dead of winter; it does give a person a lot of time to think. And that is what I did one Saturday night as I crawled into bed, pulling the blankets up to my chinny chin chin, when suddenly it hit me. Shazam, I had the answer at hand. It was my bed sheet. Of course. Why didn't I think of that sooner?

Scrambling out of bed, I found some paper and a pencil and did a rough drawing of my parachute. I wondered if da Vinci's idea came to him as he was settling in for a long winter's nap. No matter, I had the answer and it was better than his plan because I made an adaptation to meet my circumstances. And isn't that what all-good inventors do? Ha,

I would get the Nobel Prize in science as well as physics. Dad would have to build a bigger mantel over the fireplace to hold my entire collection of awards.

Long into the night I labored over my parachute diagram until I got it right. I would tie rope to the four corners of the sheet and attach the four ropes to my belt. All the pictures I'd seen of guys jumping out of planes always showed them wearing some sort of harness that was attached to the lines at the bottom of the 'chute. And the way I looked at it, tying the ropes to my belt would do the same thing. Because I only had four lines, I would put two in front and two in back. Perfect.

I also knew that a

There was a streak of the zany in my mother, not unlike Lucille Ball as Lucy Ricardo. Here, Mom dons a disguise in an obvious attempt to evade child protection authorities after she encouraged me to jump off the roof.

real parachute had to be packed properly so that it would open when you jumped out of the plane and pulled the ripcord. But I didn't have that luxury because I would only be 55-feet off the ground. And I had to take into consideration my height – 4 feet 10 inches – and the ropes' length – so there would be enough space for the sheet to open and gently bring me to the ground. Criminy, this invention stuff took a lot of thinking. If I'm 4 feet 10 inches, nah, call it 5 feet. So if I'm 5 feet, the rope should be another 5 feet, making it 10 feet of me-plus-the-

'chute, meaning I had 45 feet to deploy and descend. Hmm, not a lot of space, but that's all I had. I was confident it would work.

The next day, after church and while Mom and Oma were making Sunday dinner, I found a length of clothesline and cut it into four 5-foot pieces. Using my best Boy Scout skills, I tied each rope to a corner of the sheet and then folded it all into a neat package that I planned to attach to my backside with another small belt. I would look exactly like those guys I saw in the newsreels as they jumped over enemy territory.

As soon as dinner and the dishes were done, I ran to my room, assembled the parachute rig, strapped it on, and looked at myself in the mirror. "Not bad," I thought, "not bad at all. It's a go!"

I knew I wouldn't have the ability to actually pull a ripcord to open my 'chute, but my plan was to have the sheet laid out behind me on the roof: when I jumped, it would open overhead. At least, that's how my four-panel diagram depicted it. One, climb to the top of the roof; two, lay out the parachute behind me; three, jump; four, float to the ground. And then, of course, accept the cheers and huzzahs of the onlookers.

The one thing I hadn't done yet was to tell my parents of my parachuting plans. "No time like the present," I said to myself, strapping the rig to my behind and marching into the living room.

The old man was in his favorite chair doing what he always did on a Sunday afternoon – reading the paper. Mom was on the couch working on some knitting, and the big Philco radio in the corner was playing music.

Casually I strode into this domestic scene – but no one paid any attention. So, I reversed my tracks, whistling a little as I went. Still nothing.

"The third time's the charm," I mused to myself as I ambled closer to my father's chair. That did it. "What are you doing?" he asked as he looked over the paper at me.

"I'm getting ready to jump off the roof with my parachute," I proudly announced.

Lowering the paper, he peered at me with an incredulous look on his face. "You're what?" was all he said.

"I'm going to climb to the top of the house and jump off. But don't worry, Pop, I've got a parachute I made out of a bed sheet. See," I pointed to the pouch on my butt.

He just shook his head. "You are not going to jump off the roof. Take that thing off and put the sheet back on your bed," he said sternly and with a touch of finality in his voice.

I tried to make my case by citing the science book we were studying and the da Vinci drawing. It was no use. He wasn't hearing any of it.

Mom, however, took an interest in my invention and asked how I thought it would work. Eager to explain it all to my receptive audience, I laid it all out for her and even pulled my four-step drawing from my pocket to help my cause. She nodded her head and said she thought it might work.

"Not off my house, not off my roof," my father said firmly as he picked up the paper and went back to reading.

My mother just shifted her eyes toward the kitchen as she put her things down.

I ran to the kitchen and in a few minutes she joined me there. "What time do you get home from school tomorrow?" she asked nonchalantly.

"Three-thirty, quarter to four," I answered.

"And what time does your father go to work?"

"Er, two-thirty," I said, not quite getting it. Yet.

"There's your answer," she said as she went back to the living room.

Of course! The old man wouldn't be here. I would just postpone my grand experiment for a day. Even the atom bomb tests were delayed a few times, so what was another 24 hours? "Ha-ha, victory is mine," I reasoned as I went to my room to remake my bed.

The next day dawned cloudy and cold. I shoveled down my breakfast and during school, couldn't wait for the day to end. To heck with all this book learning. I was going to put it to real, practical use. Finally, the last bell of the day rang and I hopped on the bus, wishing the driver could read my mind and speed to my stop as quickly as possible. I half-ran, half-skied on the snow-covered road to the house and dashed to my room. Tearing the sheet off the bed, I tied the corners with the clothesline and knotted it to my belt.

"Looks like you're all set," Mom said as she entered my room. I took a deep breath and nodded.

Access to the top of the roof required climbing out a bathroom window onto the roof of the dining porch and then climbing a ladder to the main roof.

As I passed my grandmother's room, Oma pointed at the sheet and rope dragging behind me and asked, "Vas es dot?"

"He's going to use it to jump off the roof," Mom said matter-of-factly. Oma just shook her head and closed her door.

I hoisted up the big bathroom window and climbed out. The roof was covered with a thick blanket of snow that crunched as I ventured out on it. Next to the window was a ladder Dad used to get to the main roof to shovel snow after every big storm. Roofs that weren't shoveled could collapse from the weight of the snow, and the old man was very conscientious about keeping the roof over our heads, literally. Roof shoveling was a dangerous job: there was always ice underfoot and Dad had to be careful he didn't slip off. He, of course, didn't have the benefit of a trusty parachute.

"I'll watch you from the lawn," Mom said as she closed the window behind me. There was something very final about that. It meant she expected me to actually jump and not change my mind and retreat back through the bathroom. I swallowed hard as I slowly climbed the ladder to the main roof.

I had been on the roof other times with Dad when he put up our TV antenna but that was in the summer and all the leaves on the trees hid the ground from direct sight. Now the tree limbs were bare and the lawn and the road were clearly visible and seemed very far away. Clutching the bed sheet and ropes under my arm, I gingerly inched my way toward the edge of the roof. It was also windier than I had expected, and a gust from the north nearly knocked me off my feet. Out of the corner of my eye I saw my mother zipping up her coat as she came from the house. She picked her way through the snow and stood under the maple tree in the yard. Looking up at me she asked that all-important question, "Are you ready?"

I wasn't sure. Just as military planners talk of the fog of war, meaning the best-laid plans don't always occur as planned, so it was with my jumping scheme. Sure, my four-step diagram was a work of strategic art, but there were several things I hadn't taken into consideration.

First, the branches of the maple in the front yard prevented me from jumping in that direction. They'd snag me on the way down and that wouldn't be good.

Second, the opposite side of the roof had a porch roof protruding under it so that was out.

That left only one option: leaping off the side of the roof that sloped toward the road. So I didn't have the elevation I had originally planned on.

"Hurry up," my mom yelled. "It's cold out here."

Yikes. I was being heckled by my only fan, my only supporter – my mother.

Oh, and there was one more thing. The end of February is the beginning of the maple-sugaring season when the trees are tapped. At last count we had more than 350 maples on our property and we rented them out to members of the local 4-H Club. They tapped the trees and sold the syrup throughout the year and in exchange, they gave us two gallons of the finest maple syrup ever made. I mention this because at that very moment, as I was poised to jump, the 4-H kids came down the road in their big truck to collect the sap from the buckets hung on the trees.

"You're going to have an audience if you don't jump now," Mom said as she glanced down the road.

While I anticipated unending laurels and accolades for my proving Leonardo was right, I didn't anticipate a crowd of spectators like this. Even worse, they were kids I knew. I also knew they would never let me forget it if I sank like a rock into the snow. I didn't need that kind of peer attention.

With a better view of the road, I could see the truck stopping as the 4-H'ers scrambled into the woods to empty the buckets. I looked over the edge of the roof, and the ground looked really, really, really very far away – but my fate was sealed. Remember, Mom had closed the bathroom window so I knew there was only one way down... through the air.

"Come on. If you're going to jump, jump," Mom hollered. "Otherwise I'm going inside."

"Okay. I'm ready," I called back to her. Dropping my parachute, I stood at the edge of the roof and, in one swift motion, I jumped.

Sinking like a rock into the snow would have been an advantage. I plummeted like a 10-year-old wearing heavy winter boots, and in a fraction of an instant was buried armpit-deep in a snowdrift with a bed sheet draped over my head. Not hurt. But not successful, either.

By now, my mom was on the road and stood in front of me. "Are you okay? she asked.

"Yeah," I said looking at the sheet. "Did it open?"

She shook her head. "I don't think so."

Drat. Double drat.

Slowly the 4-H truck passed us as I struggled to extricate myself, wadding the sheet into a ball and shoving it into the snow. They waved and I offered a brave smile, trying to look nonchalant in my predicament.

Sliding down the snow bank onto the road, Mom undid the soggy sheet from my belt. "I'll get you a dry sheet for your bed," she said as she turned back toward the house.

"I think I know why it didn't open," I said to her as I gathered up the sheet and clotheslines. "If I recalculate the height and shorten the ropes…"

She just glanced toward the last rays of the setting sun. "Spring will be here in a few weeks and it will be time for baseball," she said, her voice trailing off.

I knew what she meant. The curse of cabin fever had been broken, and even though my one shot at parachuting into immortality was over, in my heart I knew if I tweaked my numbers I could make it work. I was sure of it. I still am.

SARAH BERGAN,
THE STATEN ISLAND SIREN

or

Don't Lose Sleep Over Me, Paul Anka

TO EACH OF US, the first bittersweet taste of love comes when we least expect it. To me it happened in the summer of 1958 when I should have been perfecting my double play combination, or at least getting the most out of the Duke Snider autographed bat I'd gotten for my birthday by learning to hit a breaking ball to the opposite field. Instead, I spent the summer overexposing my heart to the searing heat of passion, kindled by the summer sun and the desire to write the perfect love song.

As I look back on that year, I can see clearly the genesis of my vulnerability. Up to that summer, the only true love in my life was a baseball team. But not just any ball club. The team I rooted for, died for, read endless stories about, and collected pictures of, was the Brooklyn Dodgers.

My becoming a Dodger devotee went back ten years to when Sonya Milligan first came to The Maples. Sonya was the most rabid of Giants fans, and the old man was a dyed-in-the-wool Yankees supporter. At that time, the only newspapers we received were from New York, namely the *Daily News* and the *Herald Tribune*. The *Daily News* was by far the most popular because it was a tabloid crammed full of exciting photos. In fact, it was called "New York's Picture Newspaper" and, during the baseball season, it featured thrilling shots of the three local teams. Sonya was so fanatical about the Giants, she almost took affront if anyone else claimed to support the team as much as she did. Therefore, one day when she was studying a picture of Whitey Lockman making a spectacular leaping catch in the outfield, I asked why she liked the Giants. "Because they're the best team in the world. Your father likes the Yankees, the second best team in the world, so that makes you a Dodger," she decreed. So just like that, by fiat I became a Dodger fan. From then on I studied *Daily News* pictures of the Dodgers and especially reveled in victories over their dreaded National League rivals, the Giants. However, those wins over the Giants usually resulted in Sonya slugging me in the arm if I made too much of the triumph. Discretion became the better part of valor.

So I would come to know "the Boys of Summer" the way some kids knew the bumps on the back of their pet frog. Campanella, Furillo, Snider, Newcombe, Reese, Roe, Robinson, and all the others filled up every day and night of my life between April and October; and it was good.

However, when team owner Walter O'Malley announced on that fateful day, October 8, 1957, that he was going to move my beloved Dodgers to a distant planet called Los Angeles, in a barren, arid galaxy known as California, I, like thousands of other fans of "dem bums", couldn't believe it. "Say it ain't so, O'Malley! Say it ain't so," the Flatbush faithful wailed.

New York's newspapers and broadcast stations were dead-set against the idea of the Dodgers moving west. The Giants were also leaving New York behind for the West Coast but Dodgers fans were the most vocal in their opposition to this treasonous action. Those feelings were set to music and recorded by comedian Phil Foster in a song called *Let's Keep the Dodgers in Brooklyn*. In it, Phil asks, "Say, did you hear the news about what's happening in Brooklyn? We really got the blues about what's happening in Brooklyn. It ain't official yet, we hope official it don't get, but beware my friends and let me warn ya, they're thinkin' of takin' the Bums to California." And then he took it right to the big man himself. He didn't beat around the Flatbush when he pointedly sang, "Mr. Walter O'Malley, we always called you pallie, we stuck with you through thick and thin. But if you take away the Dodgers, guys like Campy, Newk and Hodges, we ain't your pal the way we been..."

But it was to no avail. The die had been cast, the Dodgers and Brooklyn would be forever separated by three times zones, three thousand miles and a million broken hearts. Worst of all, the wrecking ball did what Yankee and Giant pitchers could never do, it demolished the friendly confines of Ebbets Field, Dodger home since 1913.

So when the 1958 season opened in April, I searched my nighttime radio dial for names that would bring comfort and solace – but they weren't there. WMGM, 1050 on the AM dial in New York City, no longer carried the games I had come to rely on. The few times the Dodgers played the Pittsburgh Pirates and the static-laden signal of KDKA came filtering through the leaves of New Hampshire's maple trees, I'd shut off the radio because I couldn't bear to hear the Pirate play-by-play announcer, Bob Prince, make fun of the new sluggish, slug-less Los Angeles Dodgers. Even their name sounded odd and flat, just like their play.

Don't get me wrong. It's not that I didn't know about California or the magic it held. The halo light of our living room Sylvania surrounded Walt Disney's scrubbed-cheeked Mouseketeers and what I would later know as fantasy sprang up every time I saw Annette and Darlene.

So I spent the summer of 1958 listening to radio stations that played rock 'n' roll and didn't give many ball scores. But the summer sun has a way of adding brightness to everything, and I soon found myself in the enviable position of being a lifeguard at an all-girls summer camp.

In later years when I mentioned this vocation, hoots of delight would always come from my male friends. Hah. They didn't know the half of it.

St. Anne's Camp for girls was less than a half a mile from The Maples and the young women who populated it from late June through August were all from New York City. I found a strange sound in their words, as I'm sure they heard an unusual twang in mine.

The previous year, I had earned my Red Cross life-saving badge, learned to do artificial respiration and how to break the stranglehold a drowning person can apply on a swimming Samaritan. So I was ready when Elizabeth Kuperman, the senior adult counselor at St. Anne's, and known to everyone simply as Miss K, asked if I wanted to be the lifeguard at the camp's pond.

"We can't pay you, but there'll be lots of girls to look at," she said seriously and not without an edge of warning in her voice. I should never have trusted her because she too was a Giants' fan and rivaled Sonya in her devotion to the team. Many times I heard Miss K speak of the Giants' manager, the malevolent and cunning Leo "The Lip" Durocher, as if he were a deity. Talk like that made a Dodger fan's blood run cold despite the fact Leo managed the Dodgers many years before. That was then. This is now.

Nevertheless, Miss K didn't give me any time to answer, typical for someone who cast their allegiance with the Giants. "Fine. I don't expect any trouble, but I've got to have someone with a Red Cross badge whenever we're in the water. The job's yours," she said and handed me a large chrome whistle on a leather strap. Before I knew it, I was on the sandy banks of the pond, whistle around my neck, watching girls from eight to eighteen splashing and cavorting in a way that would have made Esther Williams want to hang up her nose clips.

The older ones, the counselors, were interesting to observe because of the way they filled out their swimsuits.

But they rarely looked my way and only spoke to ask if I had any friends who were in college. Yeah, right. College. I was just a soon-to-be-junior in high school and shook my head, no. I immediately became an outcast to these older women in search of lascivious adventure. I don't know who was more disappointed; the girls because I didn't know any college boys, or me for not looking like I was old enough to be in college myself.

However, I had met one girl the year before when the camp invited all their neighbors to the end-of-summer talent show. Her name was Sarah Bergan and when she spoke to me one early July day, I felt like I was meeting an old friend. She was blonde and wore her hair in a single braid that hung down her back, to about five inches below the nape of her neck. "I don't have to worry about getting my hair dry when I have a braid," she said.

She had a smile that went on forever, and her eyes rivaled the blue New Hampshire skies. I secretly hoped she'd get a cramp and would need me to carry her from the pond, the way Burt Lancaster carried Deborah Kerr from the surf in *From Here to Eternity*. But Miss K always made sure her charges waited a full hour between their noon meal and entering the water. Only a Giants' fan would be that calculating and cruel.

Through those hot July and August days, I soaked up the rock 'n' roll on every station my Zenith portable could find, and never once had to test my lifesaving techniques. Oh, I did give the whistle a good workout, getting the attention of little girls venturing beyond the ropes that divided the shallow end of the pond from the deeper diving area.

As the summer slowly wound down, an end-of-summer dance was planned. Girls always wanted to dance, and although I found myself caught up in the music of that summer, I was not anxious to let everyone know how poorly my feet worked. But I knew there was no escape, if for no other reason than I was the only male contact to the outside world for these child-women, and sooner or later I would have to round up some boys for their night of pleasure.

Very soon my mother got wind of the impending soirée and, after several phone calls to my pals' mothers, she assured me that I would not be alone in this rite of passage, although she did not use those exact words.

The night in question was Saturday, August 23, and when it arrived I not only brought my sacrificial friends but a portable record player and a Bill Haley album with "Rock Around the Clock" on it. I was sure Bill and I would be a hit.

With only six boys, all suffering from varying degrees of shyness, and thirty-five girls with seemingly no inhibitions, it became quite evident that if the girls wanted to dance they were going to have to dance with each other, which they did. My male companions, meanwhile, were content to drain the punch bowl and eat all the finger sandwiches in sight.

Finally, Miss K intervened. In her best Leo "the Lip" delivery, she told my friends that there would be no more refreshments until they danced with someone. This was the first time I saw food used as a weapon. It was very effective. Looking back on it now, I don't think Miss K liked the fact her Giants were playing in San Francisco any more than I liked my Dodgers being in L.A. I believe frustration put an extra edge on her words that night.

As the evening grew darker and fireflies flashed a Morse code message foreshadowing the end of summer, the music slowed and I gathered up all my courage and asked Sarah if she would dance with me.

Eagerly nodding her head, Sarah made her braid do a dance all its own. As the first scratchy bars of "Don't" by Elvis Presley warbled from my little phonograph, Sarah Bergan melted in my arms.

Now remember, this was 1958 in New Hampshire. My life, up to that point, had centered on family, church, and school, in that order, with the first two being neck and neck.

The usual suspects. Not all these lads would attend the fateful dance at the girls' camp, but for one... it became a night of doom.

While it's true I had had a crush on a little red-haired girl in the fourth grade, I'd yet to come into contact with the tingling sensation that a heart, first smitten, experiences. With the exception of the doomed *The Moon Is Blue* fiasco, lust was as foreign to me as Germany. But that night, while Elvis pleaded the sultry words "When I feel like this and I want to hold you, baby, don't say don't..." and The Jordanaires echoed the cry, I fell in love – fell like the proverbial ton of bricks – fell hard, like a hundred-pound lead weight shoved off the diving board into the pond. What I was feeling was akin to hitting a home run at Ebbets Field off the dreaded Sal Maglie. However, while I was falling, something else was rising.

With her cheek pressed to mine, her hair smelling like Prell shampoo and eyes half-closed, we shuffled back and forth to that heavy beat when I suddenly became aware of something else. There was a part of my young body that I could not control and I felt was making its presence known. Suddenly, all the sensual sounds, the sweetness of her essence and the warmth of her sun-tanned skin became a noose tightening around me. I didn't know what to do. Sarah pulled her head back for a moment, looked at me with a smile I had never, ever seen on the face of a real woman and whispered, "You're a good dancer."

I gulped a thank you and tried to steer her toward a corner where, with any luck, no one would notice anything. Elvis stopped mumbling and I tried to sidestep my way off the floor but Sarah held on to my arm as Little Anthony and the Imperials started crying on their collective pillows. She ran her hand gently up the back of my neck and I knew I was sunk. How ironic to be rising and sinking at the same time.

Before I could protest, she wound a bit of my sweat-drenched hair around her finger, the aphrodisiac Prell filled my head, and the throbbing below my belly grew more intense.

Hello Sarah, the good ship puberty has just pulled into port!

Thoughts traffic-jammed in my mind. Should I press myself close to her and risk her discovering? Or pull away and give the girls on the sidelines a shot at what was happening to me?

It was too late. Off to the side, I could see the pointed fingers and hurried, chain-reaction whispers. I had to do something, and fast.

"Let's dance outside," I blurted into Sarah's ear, took her by the hand, and rushed down the steps and into the night.

The air was damp and cool and the music wasn't so loud. But best of all, it was dark and there were no giggling girls probing me with their eyes.

Tripping over the tufts of grass, we stumbled into the dark. Our hands, sweaty from emotion and the August night, remained together. For a very long moment there was just the sound of the crickets and a distant whippoorwill. I wanted to say something great and profound but all that came out was, "Gee, your hair smells nice." Years later, I could have written an entire advertising campaign around that line.

"All right, you two. If you want to dance, you have to

dance inside," Miss K barked from the doorway. Durocher could have taken lessons from her.

We didn't go inside but instead sat on the steps where I felt more comfortable and less conspicuous. We talked of nothing and everything and I told her that the next day I was leaving for a youth retreat sponsored by my church and that I hoped to see her before the camp closed for the season.

At that point, two tittering girls came bouncing down the steps and told Sarah she was wanted inside.

When she returned, she was crying and told me her friends said she shouldn't be with me because I could get her in a lot of trouble. Sobbing a soggy "good night", she ran to the huge bunkhouse where the girls slept.

What a splash of cold water that was! Me? Get a girl in trouble? "I'm a Lutheran/Methodist," I thought. "We don't get girls in trouble! Honest. Ask anyone!" But it was too late. I had been stabbed with the rapier of my teenage carnal appetites. I couldn't go back into that room, not with all those eyes. So I told anyone who would listen that I had to leave to get ready for my trip the next day.

The walk home was the longest and darkest of my life. The girl of my dreams would forever think of me as a sex-driven monster right out of a cheap and tawdry novel. Only God knew how many perverts like me she had encountered in the New York jungle, and now she had found one in New Hampshire, too.

When I returned from the retreat five days later, I knew I had to face her. It would be difficult to talk with all those prying eyes around but it had to be done. Putting on my bravest smile, I walked to the pond one last time.

The camp was closing up. In fact, the youngest girls had already been sent home by train, armed to invade New York City with half-sewn leather wallets and dried clover leaves pressed between crumpled sheets of waxed paper.

As I came over the hill with its scrub pine trees and

rambling blueberry bushes, I saw Sarah and a bunch of other girls constructing a cinderblock fireplace on the sand by the pond. Each year, the older girls worked on a project everyone could enjoy the next season. This year it was a fireplace, site of future cookouts.

There were a few giggles as I approached and I heard someone say, "Hey, Sarah, look who's here."

She finished putting her initials in the wet cement and walked toward me with that braid dancing behind her. She squinted in the sun as she looked at me, my eyes hidden behind dark aviator sunglasses.

"I'm leaving tomorrow but if you'd like to write, I'd love to hear from you," she said with a smile that crinkled up her nose.

My heart stopped and I'm sure a million brain cells died from lack of oxygen at that moment. She said the word... love. She'd love to hear from me. "Maybe things weren't so bad after all," I thought.

"I'll get some paper," she said as she picked her beach bag out of the sand and with a heavy backhand slant, printed her name and address on a piece of robin's-egg-blue stationery. But I didn't need the paper. I tattooed her name and Staten Island street address on the back of my eyelids, and I can still see them as clearly as I did on that late August day. Now I knew why a songwriter said, "I'll take Manhattan, the Bronx and Staten Island, too": because he knew Sarah Bergan lived there!

The next morning I stood in the dirt driveway at The Maples, tossing a tattered baseball into the air and catching it, impatiently waiting for the camp bus to rattle by with its precious cargo. I heard it before I saw it. Windows full of tanned faces, it chugged up the hill in a cloud of dust, exhaust fumes and waving hands. Sarah was leaning out the rear window and called, "Don't forget to write," over the sound of the straining engine. I gave my handsomest smile and waved back, watching the bus until it went around the bend by the big maple tree, and was out of sight.

That afternoon I walked to the now-silent pond and traced her initials in the fireplace with my finger. I wondered how I would ever make it through the winter. A bullfrog burped his condolences.

School started right after Labor Day, so the last days of August were filled with buying new chinos, three-ringed notebook paper, and lots of stamps for the letters I would write.

On September 3, a letter came for me. I didn't need to see the New York postmark to know who sent it. The heavy backhand slant sang, Sarah Bergan. As I ran to my attic bedroom to read and dream, I saw the stamp was upside down. Even in the boonies of New Hampshire we had heard of such things. Either a stamp upside down is a mistake or ... it means the sender is in love with you. But that wasn't all! Along the edge of the back flap of the envelope were the small letters, "s.w.a.k.," sealed with a kiss. MY GOD!! I was being kissed long distance from New York!

Had the Angel of Death flown through my window that afternoon, I would have been the happiest corpse in the world.

I answered in detail all that I was doing and how much I missed her. Listening to Dion and the Belmonts along with Paul Anka sharpened my flair for the dramatic and I snatched phrases from their songs to express the feelings of my soul. Then something hit me: Why not write my own song to show Sarah how I really feel? That's it! I'll write the greatest love song in the world! After all, when you're sixteen and dreams are erupting in your heart, anything is possible.

I envisioned Buddy Holly or the Everly Brothers or, dare I say it, Elvis, doing my song. Thoughts of Dick Clark introducing me on *American Bandstand* as the writer of the nation's Number 1 hit song bopped in my head. I could see myself telling the cheering masses how Sarah Bergan danced into my life and inspired me. Love and success would be mine before I graduated high school.

There were just a few things I had to do before I cashed those royalty checks. The first was getting music for my epic poem of love.

Before I could say "Hoagy Carmichael!" the answer grabbed me by the eyeballs. A small one-inch ad in a magazine I was reading said it all: "Songwriters Wanted! We'll put music to your words. You could earn big dollars and your song could be a hit! Free evaluation of your poem. Crown Music Company, New York, New York."

It was almost more than I could believe. Someone was actually advertising for songwriters! America was truly the land of opportunity. It took me less than twenty minutes to complete the classic that I was sure would engrave my name on the steps of Tin Pan Alley forever.

"I'll bet I could just send this to her and she'd be on the next train to New Hampshire, begging me to get her into trouble," I smugly thought. "And when this gets played on all the New York radio stations, Sarah will see that I am not a wild-eyed sex maniac. No, I am an artist!"

Within five days, I got a letter from my altruistic fellow songwriters in New York. It said in part, "We have carefully examined your lyrics and will be glad to collaborate with you..."

They also let me know that this collaboration would result in a lead sheet with my lyrics and a piano accompaniment for a mere thirty-nine dollars. Thirty-nine dollars? In 1958, that was a king's ransom to a kid of sixteen. But then I considered the possible rewards...maybe $10,000, perhaps $20,000 in royalties plus the undying love of the most wonderful, beautiful braid-bedecked girl in the world.

There really wasn't any question about my decision. "I'll do it," I said. "I'll do it for us, Sarah and me!"

The next step was getting the money, something I never had a lot of. But with a little saving here and skipping lunch there, I was able to swing it. And just in time, too, because my brother songwriters at Crown were really starting to push for that money. Every day, a letter came assuring me that they would do all they could to help me have a hit – if I would only send them the money to get the ball rolling. Or note playing. Or whatever.

They went so far as to enclose a copy of a letter from a radio station in Bennettsville, South Carolina. Written by the program director, he told a woman in Logansport, Indiana, that the song she sent to the station had, "a definite chance of becoming a real bomb."

In a scrawl across the bottom of the page, someone at Crown Music assured me that "this is what a big radio station thought of one of the songs for which we composed the music!"

I looked at that letter; confident my song for Sarah could be a bomb, too. At least I hoped so.

Naturally, I knew a bomb was something dropped from a plane and created a big explosion. So that's what I thought the Crown boys meant, a song that would explode all over the land. Oh, what a fool I was. Several years later when I got into broadcasting, I learned that a song or record referred to as a "bomb" is the worst of the worst and would never be played on the air. Another lesson I learned that summer is what "chutzpah" means. Not only did my colleagues at Crown display a great deal of it, they charged me thirty-nine dollars for the lesson and I eagerly handed over the cash. Welcome to life, kid.

My next hurdle was getting the money to New York. I knew I couldn't send cash and in those days hardly anyone had a checking account, so I went to the post office for a money order.

Ordinarily this would be an easy matter, but when you live in a small town like Spofford, and the postmistress knows everyone's business, it becomes a bit more difficult. At least it seemed that way to my paranoid, 16-year-old mind. For one thing, I just couldn't let my parents know that their son was spending thirty-nine dollars to have a song written for his girlfriend in New York. No, this had to be done on the q.t.

Buying a money order from someone you know, but don't want them to know why you're buying it, can be tricky. Or so I thought. I lived in constant fear that the postmistress would spill everything to my dad.

"Mornin', Fred. Your son bought a money order for thirty-nine dollars the other day," I could hear her say. "You'd better have that boy checked. I think he's having a song written for that Bergan girl in New York. He'll get her in trouble, you mark my words." My sleepless nights were filled with these dark visions.

Be that as it may, it had to be done. Taking a deep breath, I grabbed my thirty-nine dollars and walked into the little country post office, not unlike Marshal Dillon walking into the Long Branch and ordering a shot of redeye.

The place was empty and Mrs. Post, the postmistress, was doing postal things behind the bars of a window with the words, "Money Orders," over it. Her constant companion, a smoldering Camel cigarette, was between her fingers and she looked over her glasses at me as I made my request.

"Hi, Mrs. Post. I'd like a money order for thirty-nine dollars please," I chirped.

"Thirty-nine dollars," she mumbled and began to fill out the blue postcard-size form. My underarms were getting very damp. Suddenly, two women came in to pick up their mail and Mrs. Post started a lengthy conversation about some new people who had just moved into a camp on the lake and then segued into the latest winners at the Hinsdale racetrack. That is when I realized I had nothing to worry about; she probably wouldn't even remember this transaction. I slid the crumpled bills toward her and she quickly counted them as she handed me the money order and brushed away the gray ash from her Camel.

Quickly retreating to a counter at the back of the small room, I stuffed the money order and a pound of my heart into an envelope and sent it off to New York.

Four days later, I got my contract from Crown and the assurance that, within the next two weeks, I would get my song and be on my way to fame and, if all went well, fortune.

All this mail from New York didn't escape the ever-watchful eye of my mom and she wanted to know what Crown Music Company wanted with me. I artfully said that I was writing to them for some music. Her eyes lit up and she asked if I was going to start playing the piano again. "Yeah, maybe," I said as I went to my room, clutching the latest letter from my collaborators. In this one, they tried to sell me a thousand copies of my song for fifty dollars and then they'd distribute these copies to publishers, record companies and singers for an additional seventy-five dollars. I quickly saw myself becoming an indentured servant to Crown Music Company.

Another letter came from Staten Island and Sarah said she would be in the audience for the *Dick Clark Saturday Night Beechnut Show* on ABC-TV on the second Saturday of October. "Be sure to look for me. I'll wave to you," she said, and I imagined the crinkled nose and smile.

Television reception in New Hampshire in the fifties was marginal at best. We always had TV snow in our living room twelve months of the year. So that Saturday night, I searched a sea of faces through an electronic blizzard, looking for blue eyes in a black-and-white world, and a braid that danced. I found neither. After the program, I went to my room and wrote Sarah the letter I had been waiting to write for weeks.

Pouring out my heart, I detailed how I really felt about her and, to prove it, I had written a song just for her and I knew it would be played on radio stations all across the country. I even included the lyrics to the song. That would be the clincher. "Sarah Bergan is mine," I thought smugly. I affixed my upside-down stamp and mailed the letter

Monday morning.

That next week was hell. I didn't know what I wanted more, a letter from Sarah or the song from Crown. The music came first in a very B I G envelope. It was waiting for me on the dining room table when I got home from school. "God, how do I explain this?" I wondered.

"Are you going to play your new music?" my mother asked.

"Yeah, I'll get to it," I cavalierly answered as I ran to my room.

Tearing open the envelope, I just sat and looked at the lead sheet for the longest time. It was a complete piano and voice arrangement, fully harmonized for both hands. In addition, it had my name on it as author, and a copyright of 1958. I was a songwriter, a milestone in my young life and soon it would become a millstone.

Two days later I got a letter from Staten Island. As I drank in the words the way a man dying of thirst would consume a cup of cold water, I couldn't believe my eyes. The love of my life, my Helen of Troy, my soul and inspiration, had shown my letter to her BOYFRIEND!

Her boyfriend? I didn't even know she had a boyfriend. Naturally, he didn't like the song and ordered her not to write to me anymore. Therefore, Sarah wrote, "This will be my last letter..."

I felt like a truck had hit me. I'd just spent thirty-nine hard-earned dollars and poured out my soul! For what? To be told by Sarah Bergan's indifference that I was a fool? Yikes. That's what I was. A fool. A fool for love. It sounded like something I'd heard in a song. It appeared Father Conklin was right after all; a woman's a worrisome thing who'll leave ya to sing the blues in the night...

For a while I kept getting letters from Crown Music, but I never opened them. And despite Sarah saying she'd never write again, I got a few more notes from Staten Island, too.

They were mostly about her family, school projects and TV shows she liked. By the following April they stopped coming.

The next summer I was working at a grocery store and didn't have time for lifesaving, or songwriting, or anything romantic. It was just as well, because Sarah Bergan didn't make it to Saint Anne's that summer and I never saw her again.

One afternoon, when no one was in the house, I pulled my song from the drawer where I'd stashed it many months before, and played it on the piano. My song wasn't bad. It had a nice melody, not unlike Paul Anka's "You Are My Destiny." If I had been on *Bandstand*, I would have given it a seventy. Maybe an eighty. It would have been a good song to dance close to. I wondered what Sarah Bergan would have given it had she heard it.

By 1959 the Dodgers were world champions and would repeat that feat several more times. Over the years I have thought about Sarah and wondered what became of her. Did any other boy ever write her a song? I hope so and I hope it was a gold record hit. She deserved it.

PROST!

or

Oma and Gin – Not a Good Mix

S UMMER PEOPLE LIKED TO DRINK.
That's all there is to say. It is the stone-cold truth and
I'm not talking about sipping the sweet, mountain-borne spring
water that streamed from our taps. Nope. They were partial
to anything that had a proof number on its label. Bourbon,
Scotch, rye, rum, gin, vodka, port, sherry, as well as beer
and ale all flowed freely on the cool porches and just about
everywhere else at The Maples.

All of that imbibing made for interesting, and
occasionally, heated conversation about everything, including
politics and religion, any time of the day or night. But mainly
the sampling of spirits occurred during evening card games
with, naturally, gin rummy being the most popular.

We never had a state liquor license so we couldn't sell
anyone a drink but there was nothing wrong with serving a
guest anything they brought with them. On more than one
occasion when the old man picked up guests at the train
station in Brattleboro, the new arrival would inquire about
the availability of spirits. Then Dad would explain about The
Maples' lack of a liquor license, and the freedom of guests
to indulge in his or her own tastes. This inevitably led to a
request to stop at ye old local schnapps shoppe to purchase an
adequate supply. So he did.

About the only time booze wasn't poured was during breakfast and that was not a hard and fast rule. There were occasions when morning came a tad too early for a previously inebriated guest, and the customary two aspirins or plop-plop-fizz-fizz of an Alka-Seltzer just didn't do the trick. That's when the liquored lamentations went out for something called the "hair of the dog."

When you are six years old, everything is very literal, especially words, and the subtlety of nuance and alternate meaning is yet to be appreciated. Or at least, that's the way it was with me. True, I knew the phrase "get lost" really didn't mean wandering out into the forest never to be seen again. Geeze, any kid knew that. But hair of the dog was something I took at face, or fur, value.

The first time I heard the phrase, it was softly uttered by a certain Mr. Dom LaGigglia of Jersey City, New Jersey, on the dining porch and he was gripping the tablecloth with one hand while clutching the water glass I had just put down with his other paw. My mother was in the process of placing a plate of scrambled eggs and toast in front of him and, from his reaction to it, one would have thought it was a bowl of underdone newt eyes.

"Please, Marion, no food. Not this morning. What I really need is some hair of the dog," he moaned with more than a little urgency.

"What you need is a cup of hot coffee," his wife Yvonne said without much sympathy. "Just bring him some coffee, he'll be fine," she instructed Mom.

"No, no, that won't work," he stated firmly as he continued to hold onto the tablecloth as if it were a lifeline he dare not release.

"I told you to take it easy last night, but you wouldn't listen. Oh no, mister I-can-drink-anyone-under-the-table just had to keep at it," Yvonne said with a tightness in her voice.

My mother looked at me and tilted her head toward the

kitchen. I knew that look and that tilt. It always meant for me to scram because something was happening that she didn't want me to hear.

"Just a little hair of the dog will fix everything," he pleaded, looking at my mom, a trembling smile at the corner of his mouth.

"Hair of the dog? Why would anyone want that?" I thought to myself. I'd gotten dog hair in my mouth on a few occasions, usually when I was combing my dog, Rover, or giving him a hug, and it was nasty stuff. Wanting some at the breakfast table was a mystery to me. "Shall I get Rover?" I asked. Before Mom could answer, big Dom burst into laughter.

"Yvonne, honey, do you hear that? The kid thinks I want to bite his dog," he howled.

"No," my mother said firmly, "just take this back to the kitchen," and she handed me Dom's plate.

"What's going on out there?" the old man asked and, seeing the plate of eggs on my tray, he added, "Who doesn't like the eggs?"

"It's Mr. LaGigglia and he wants some of Rover's hair," I said as I slid the plate onto the counter.

He looked at me as if I had just sprouted a second head covered with those newt eyes. "What are you talking about?"

Just then my mother came into the kitchen and he turned his inquisition to her. "What is he talking about? There's dog hair in someone's food? That dog has to stay outside when we have people here," he said inspecting the plate of eggs for any trace of Rover's coat.

My mother took the plate from Dad. "No, there's nothing wrong with the eggs. It's Dom LaGigglia and he had a little too much last night and now wants, you know, some hair of the dog. What was he drinking? I think it was whiskey," she said as she glanced at the array of bottles at far end of the counter. Taking a tumbler from a cabinet she poured it half-full of amber liquid and put it on my tray.

"Take him this," she instructed.

Mr. LaGigglia was still giggling, in a painful way, as I approached his table. Something told me it would be funny if I said something funny so, as I placed the glass in front of him, I whispered, "From Rover."

It worked. He threw his head back and laughed so hard he nearly tipped over backwards. His wife reached out and grabbed his arm to steady him. "Dominic," she screamed. "That's rich," he guffawed as he dabbed his eyes with a napkin and then drank the entire glass in one gulp. Coughing, he pounded his fist on the table and said to me, "Good Rover!"

I still didn't know what the hair of a dog had to do with everything but it sure was a hit.

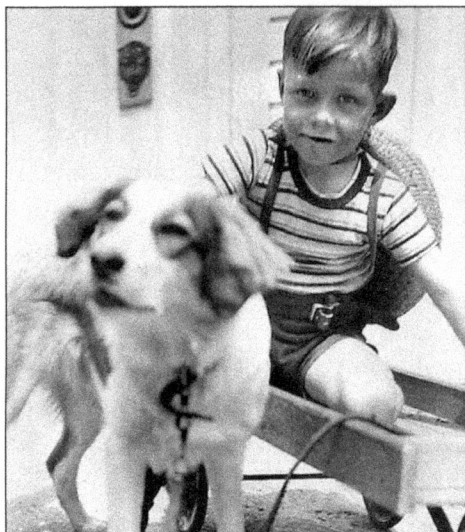

He didn't look like much, but Rover was our best source for hair of the dog.

The man at the next table, however, was about to enlighten me.

It was Dr. Irving Mann, a physician who trained at Harvard Medical School and was the go-to guy to settle bets about anything medical.

Dr. Mann had a look of Albert Einstein about him. There was a shock of white hair that sort of wandered across his head, and he had a bushy gray mustache and wore thin, wire-rimmed glasses. "You see, Clifford, 'hair of the dog' is a term people use when they've had too much alcohol to drink and they think having more will sober them up," he intoned in a scholarly way. "And there is some merit to that theory," he added. "What Mr. LaGigglia requested is actually a shortened version of the original phrase that is, 'the hair of the dog that bit you.'

"It dates to the time of Shakespeare because back then it was believed that if a person was bitten by a dog, especially a rabid dog, putting some hairs from the animal on the wound would prevent anything evil from happening, such as infection. Obviously, that was just a fable and has no actual application today."

"Oh, fer Christ sake, can it, will ya," big Dom bellowed. "We're trying to have breakfast here, not attend one of your goddamn lectures," he added pointing his finger at the doc.

Suddenly breakfast was becoming one of the late night card games when the subject of politics came up.

"But the boy wants to know," the doctor calmly said, "and I am merely answering his question. It's healthy."

"I'm gonna need a pack of dogs before the morning's done," Dom mumbled as he put his head in his hands.

Dr. Mann continued. "Clifford, you will observe that Mr. LaGigglia is suffering from a common ailment, a hangover. It is the consequence of consuming too much alcohol, which results in poisoning by the toxic chemicals into which alcohol is converted by the body. I am sure Mr. LaGigglia is experiencing dehydration and his electrolytes, blood glucose, and B-vitamins are all, how should I say it, out of whack.

"It should be noted that the symptoms of a hangover are similar to those of withdrawal from any powerful drug, namely a throbbing headache, nausea, and possible vomiting. Have you been sick this morning, Mr. LaGigglia?" he asked leaning toward Dom.

"Yeah, sick of hearing your big mouth," came the replay.

"It can affect the nerves, too," the doc said with a wry smile. "But to my point; consuming more alcohol, the hair of the dog, might actually help by blunting some of the hangover symptoms. A few of my colleagues agree."

He took a sip of ice water, dabbed his napkin in the glass and ran the wet cloth across his mouth as if to wipe away all the words he just spoke, and then got up from the table. "I hope you feel better, Mr. LaGigglia. I bid you all a good morning," he said cheerfully and left the dining porch.

"Quack," Dom muttered.

"Shhhhh!" His wife hissed loudly.

Well, it wasn't often that we got a lecture from a Harvard man for breakfast, but at least I knew what the hair of the dog meant and Rover was off the hook.

THIS WAS NOT the first time Dr. Mann inserted his medical knowledge and opinions into events around him. While he was a good source of information to settle bar bets late at night, some of the summer people called him Dr. Buttinski, referring to his penchant for poking his proboscis into the business of others. But the truth is, he earned some respect when he resolved one particular midnight argument.

I always went to bed around 10:30 but my room was adjacent to the big-screened porch where everyone gathered in the evening to talk, drink, and play cards. Illuminated by kerosene hurricane lamps, it was the most popular spot in the house because there was always a soft breeze to cool even the sultriest of nights. So every night I'd be lulled to sleep by the mingling of voices, clinking glasses, and laughter. That also meant I could be aroused from sleep when the whisky-and gin-fueled political and religious disputes flared up.

This particular night I was probably dreaming about riding the range with Roy Rogers and Trigger, when the decibel of voices reached the wake-up level. Apparently, two guests had gotten unto an argument over whether coconut milk could be used to replace human blood. One gentleman said he had read an article in *The New York Times* that said it was possible and the other gentleman accused the first gentleman of being an ass and not knowing what he was talking about. Despite the efforts of their wives to silence them and take them to bed, the deliberation raged on. Finally, one of them suggested they ask Dr. Mann because he was Mr. Know-It-All when it came to medicine. Unfortunately, the good doctor had retired hours earlier, keeping with his belief that early to bed and early to rise meant there would never be red in his eyes.

As the master of the house, my old man said it wasn't right to summon a guest from his bed just to settle a harebrained argument. But there was no stopping the drunken debaters. They both demanded an answer. So Mom was dispatched to knock on the doctor's door and see if he would join the gang on the porch. Only his opinion would bring peace to the house that night.

A few minutes later he appeared, wrapped in a bathrobe, floppy slippers on his feet, and his normally wild thatch of hair even wilder and thatchier.

Both sides presented their case for and against coconut milk as a substitute for human blood. Sitting in a comfortable wicker chair, the doc listened to the pros and cons, not unlike the way King David must have listened to the disagreements of his people.

After a long moment he cleared his throat and delivered his verdict. *The New York Times* was right. It had been recently discovered, during World War II, that in an emergency, the milky water inside a young coconut could be used to take the place of human plasma. He even knew one of the researchers mentioned in the article. The victor shouted great huzzahs into the night and drank a celebratory drink, while the vanquished wondered how it was possible for coconut milk or juice or whatever it was called to take the place of blood. He couldn't understand it. But that ended the night and everyone went to bed, including me, and I think the rest of my dreams were about Dracula climbing palm trees only to break his teeth while trying to sink them into a coconut. I'm sure I even dreamed Bela Lugosi was wearing a grass skirt. It wasn't a pretty sight.

Despite the midnight heroics, Dr. Mann was more often considered by the summer people as someone who should just keep his mouth shut. Especially when he would criticize the eating habits of his fellow guests – while they were dining. In retrospect, he was ahead of his time. But back then, in a very meat-and-potatoes world, questioning what others were putting in their mouths could result in your mouth getting punched. He would constantly ask why everyone felt it necessary to consume so much animal protein, especially when he could prove that eating pork and beef was a sure way to die young. A typical response was a wish for that to happen to him at that moment. But criticism never deterred his zeal to convince everyone to eat better. And heaven help the person he spied putting salt on their food or sugar in their coffee. He'd launch into a lecture on how the Chinese knew, five-thousand years ago, that salt is bad for the heart, and that using refined white sugar throws the body out of kilter.

It was after one of his impromptu lectures on nutrition that the old man called him aside and asked him to keep his opinions about food to himself – he was disturbing the other guests who were trying to relax and enjoy themselves. The doc responded that he felt it was his duty to warn people about their poor eating habits, and he hoped we would stop serving meat and only dish up vegetables for everyone. I'm sure our chickens cheered that remark, but the old man said it wouldn't happen and so Dr. Mann departed, never to return. If chickens could cry, they must have shed a tear or two that day.

That was also the summer I learned to mix adult beverages. It started the same way my collecting chicken heads started: I watched the old man. When making a bunch of highballs for some guests, he dropped ice cubes in a glass, added whiskey, topped it off with club soda and stirred things up with a glass rod. There were eight more glasses to fill, and he said I should do exactly what he did. So I did. True, I had to stand on a stool to reach the counter, and my first couple of pours resulted in spills. But he said as long as I spilled the soda and not the whiskey, everything would be okay.

Soon I was mixing drinks on a regular basis. I'm certain if it were today and word got out what I was doing, some bleeding-heart social service organization would throw my parents in jail and put me into big-time counseling for the rest of my life. But just as it was a meat-and-potato age as far as food was concerned, it was a cocktail-highball age when it came to drinks.

One hot July night the screened porch was especially lively with new arrivals sharing their horror stories of riding a train from Grand Central Station to Brattleboro with no air conditioning and windows that wouldn't open. Dad was working at the AO, Mom was entertaining the guests, Oma was making little cheese-and-liverwurst sandwiches, and I was tending bar. The guests were especially thirsty and I was very busy. There was a heated pinochle game on the dining porch and the players demanded constant refills. At one point I brought a fresh round of highballs to the table and a rotund German gentleman everyone called "Uncle" took a sip from his glass and said in a thick accent, "Clifford, next time you make me a highball, use a little more high and a little less ball." The whole room erupted in laughter but I had no idea what he was talking about. Was this going to be hair of the dog all over again? Then one of the other players leaned over to me and explained he meant more whiskey and less soda. Got it.

While too much alcohol might result in spirited conversations and raised voices, a simple request for a certain dinner wine could produce raised eyebrows.

THE LITTLE AD we ran in New York newspapers tended to get lost among the larger, gaudier advertising for resorts in the Catskills in upstate New York and Pennsylvania's Pocono Mountains. It was tough to compete with Grossinger's, the Concord or even the smaller Borscht Belt hotels, bungalows,

91

inns and camps scattered throughout the mountains along the Hudson River. Besides, they were a lot closer to New York City and thus required less travel. They also offered top entertainment: Red Buttons, Shecky Greene, Henny Youngman and other show biz luminaries performed there. All The Maples had was me, the youngest bartender in captivity.

So most of our guests were there because of word-of-mouth advertising. Someone would tell someone who would stay and tell someone else about the quirky little inn nestled in the foothills of New Hampshire.

Therefore, it wasn't a surprise when Mom got a call from a man named Jimmy Ryan who said he was a good friend of Jack and Ruth Sullivan. They worked with Dad back in the New York days and had been our guests many times. Jimmy said he and his wife, Liz, wanted to spend a long weekend and reservations were made. Some days later, the Ryans arrived and, being the chief bellboy, as well as the waiter-busboy, head chicken-head-collector, and occasional bartender, I showed them to their room. There was even a shiny quarter tip for my time, thank you very much.

That summer a family named Clooney was also our guests, along with Mrs. Clooney's father, whom everyone called "Grandpa McCrea." A couple of days after the Ryans arrived, Grandpa McCrea went up to my mom and said, "Missis, there's somthin' fishy about them two in the room next to mine." Mom asked what was wrong and the old man said, "They spend too much time in there. It's not right. They should be out in the fresh air. It's not right they spend so much time in the bedroom. It's not natural. And there's laughin' at night, too. I'm tellin' ya, somethin's wrong."

Mom dismissed Grandpa's observations, but a few days later he reported he saw the Ryans holding hands and kissing down by the brook, "In broad daylight. I'm tellin' ya, it's not natural."

On the last night of their stay, Jimmy Ryan asked if he

and Liz could have their supper on the screened porch, away from the other guests. He also produced a bottle of French white wine with instructions that it be properly chilled and served with their dinner.

Wine, French or otherwise, was something rarely seen or served at The Maples. Occasionally a bottle of champagne was uncorked, but only for special dinners such as Christmas or my parents' wedding anniversary. So that night, I turned a few heads as I carried the silver tray with the wine bottle and two stemmed glasses past the other diners and delivered it to a small table at the far end of the porch.

"Last time I saw a bottle that big was when Mrs. Roosevelt christened a battleship," some wag commented and the room filled with raucous laughter.

If the secluded couple heard the comment, they paid no attention. They seemed to be lost in each other's company. They just picked at the poached chicken breast and garden fresh vegetables I served them. When the wine was gone, they quietly exited through a side door so they wouldn't have to walk the gauntlet of the other guests on the dining porch. And slowly they strolled, hand in hand, down the dirt road with fireflies lighting the way.

The next day they were gone, but not before I got another quarter for taking their bags to the car. As far as I was concerned, with tips like that they could have stayed all summer.

Nothing more was said about them or their penchant for staying in their room when other guests were out playing badminton or horseshoes or canasta. But the following summer, Jack Sullivan and his wife came up for a week and Mom thanked them for recommending the place to Jimmy Ryan and his wife.

"Jimmy Ryan's not married," Jack said.

"Oh, yes, he is," Mom responded. "He was here with his wife, Liz. She was very nice, sweet and quiet," Mom added.

Jack looked puzzled. "But Marion, he's not married. I should know, I work with him. We're on the same bowling team. God knows, Ruth's been trying to fix him up with one of her friends, but Jimmy's a confirmed bachelor." He paused for a moment and waved his hand in the air. "Hold it a second. Did you say the lady's name was Liz? That's his secretary! Liz Connolly! Hey, Ruth, Jimmy Ryan's got a girlfriend and he brought her up here, that dog," he said with a lusty laugh.

But to my mother, it was no laughing matter. Her face turned pale. "Oh, my God, Grandpa McCrea was right. There was something wrong with them. They weren't married," she said shaking her head. "They committed adultery under our roof," she added, looking up the stairs to where the bedrooms were and where the evil deed was done, probably more than once.

Jack may have had a good laugh when he heard the story, but Mom never got over the incident and she wanted to ask for a marriage license whenever new couples checked in. Dad talked her out of it, but she didn't like the idea that, at least once, The Maples had become a house of ill repute.

IN ADDITION to consuming copious amounts of alcohol, the summer people liked playing games. At night it was cards, but during the day they enjoyed bocce on the front lawn, badminton on the lower lawn, as well as horseshoes next to the side porch where fans would raise a glass of something cool and toast the combatants. When kids were around, the men could be coaxed into a ragtag round of stickball on the dirt road that ran past the house. A maple sapling became first base; a pile of stones in the middle of the road was second, and third was usually the blackberry patch on the edge of the garden. Running past third, however, could result in some serious scratches, and digging a ball out of a tangle of weeds at the edge of the road might result in a rash of poison ivy up to the elbow, a hindrance never encountered on the mean streets

94

of New York where most players learned the game.

And so it was on a sultry Saturday afternoon in July that a stickball game was being played on the dusty road. It was the kids – Sonya, my cousins Walter and Marge, and myself – versus the men – my dad, Uncle Walter, and two other guys. We were, as they say, cleaning their clocks, thanks to Sonya's rocket line drives far down the road, and her dazzling leaping catches. She certainly could have beaten the old guys all by herself. But after a few innings with the score "a lot" to "not so much," the men gave up and

Party like it's 1958. Summer people would put on funny hats and consume large amounts of adult beverages at any occasion including Robert's seventh birthday party.

suggested we all adjourn to the screened porch for something cool to drink. The old man hollered for everyone to "wash good" so as not to spread the dreaded poison ivy around the dinner table.

While we kids hooked up the garden hose and started spraying each other, the men trudged into the house in search of that cold drink, i.e., beer and martinis. Uncle Walter led the way to the refrigerator in the kitchen and quickly removed every ice tray in the freezer. Filling a pitcher, he took a large bottle of gin from the sideboard and proceeded to pour it over the ice. Dad took several bottle of beer from the fridge and I grabbed four Cokes for my teammates.

While all the beverage wrangling was going on, Oma

was slaving over the hot stove getting the lunch together. No mater how warm the weather, she was in her element preparing something to eat. That day she was working three cast iron frying pans filled with plump hamburgers as well as a Dutch oven bubbling with hot oil into which she was plopping handfuls of crinkle-cut potatoes for fries. Even in winter, the kitchen would be hot, and this afternoon it was almost like a blast furnace. But that didn't deter Oma. She was a trained cook and knew the rigors of a hot stove. Stoically, she wiped her brow with the long apron she was wearing and continued with the task at hand.

Mom was starting to set the tables in the dining room, and she told me to get out of my wet clothes and help her. Meanwhile, Uncle Walter had filled a large silver tray with water glasses and his big iced pitcher of gin. It should be noted that Walter Vogel was proud of his martinis. Every afternoon and evening he would offer anyone who wanted to join him in what he said was the perfect martini. He called it the Lamont Cranston martini and always got laughs when he described how it was made. For the uninitiated, Lamont Cranston was the civilian identity of "The Shadow," a popular pulp fiction and radio crime fighter of the 1930s and 1940s who was able to become an invisible avenger because he possessed the mysterious power to cloud men's minds so they could not see him. Capitalizing on that concept, Walter's Lamont Cranston martini consisted of as much gin as a clear glass pitcher would hold and then he would carefully take a bottle of Italian vermouth and place it between a light source and the pitcher so, as he put it, "the shadow of the vermouth falls across the gin, and as a result the contents of the pitcher will cloud men's minds!"

The Lamont Cranston was always served in chilled, stemmed glasses with an olive. But this day, speed was of the essence for his thirsty pals on the porch and he grabbed water glasses instead of the more traditional martini glasses.

Walking past Oma at the stove, he stopped and in a loud voice said, "Oma. Schwitzen?" meaning, are you sweating? Turning with one hand on her hip and the other wiping her forehead, she nodded. "Ja, Walter, schwitzen viel." She was sweating a lot. Then he asked the fateful question, "Oma, wollen einen trinken?" Did she want a drink? She nodded her head. "Ja." He held out the tray and she lifted the pitcher and filled one of the glasses to the brim. The old lady must have thought it was just ice water because she lifted it to her lips, tilted her head back, and drank it down in one swallow.

That's when it hit her, the six ounces of straight gin. Her eyes got big, she turned and lurched toward a chair and plopped down. Seeing the look on her face, Walter called to my mother. "Marion, I think Oma's going to pass out!" Before Mom could render any assistance, Oma was sliding to the floor. It was like a scene from a Warner Bros. cartoon where Bugs Bunny does something to Elmer Fudd and poor Elmer becomes like jelly and oozes into a puddle. Mom and Dad rushed in and tried to help her to her feet, but her legs were as limp as wet noodles. "Take her to her room," my mother ordered and the old man swept Oma into his arms and rushed upstairs. "Walter, you should know better than to give her one of your martinis," Mom scolded as she quickly took a frying pan-full of hamburgers off the stove just before they started to burn.

Sheepishly, Walter headed toward the porch but managed to announce to everyone, "The Shadow strikes again. Get 'em while they're cold, folks – lunch might be delayed!"

Oma was out like a light and Mom put a cold compress on her head. We took turns checking on her through the afternoon and evening but she was sleeping peacefully and didn't stir until the next morning. A good Lamont Cranston could not only cloud men's minds, it would definitely knock a little old German lady for a loop.

THE STORK COMETH

or

Oh, Brother!

AUGUST 25TH, 1951, was warm, humid and rainy. In a word, close. The dream I was dreaming had me at the bottom of a deep well and the sound of a ringing telephone urged me to reach the surface before I drowned. It was 8:30 A.M.

As in most 1950s homes, there was only one phone and ours was in the kitchen, at least five miles from my bedroom and equally far from the bottom of that well. So responding to the phone and stopping the ringing took about an hour, or so it seemed.

When I reached the phone and finally said, hello, I heard my dad say, "Clifford? You have a brother. Your mother is fine. Tell Oma everything is okay. Okay? I'll be home in a little while."

I said okay and hung up. Wow, a brother.

The night before, Dad and I went to the Keene Drive-In Theater to see a Tarzan double-feature, but about halfway through the second film, *Tarzan's Peril*, starring Lex Barker, my favorite Lord of the Jungle, the old man said it was time to go. He had been smoking one Lucky Strike after another and, even though the windows of our 1950 Chevy were rolled down that summer night, I felt like I had inhaled at least a dozen of the cigarettes myself and was feeling a little woozy. Consequently I didn't protest our leaving, even though it meant I wouldn't find out what peril Lord Greystoke was in. Dad had been nervous ever since he left Mom at the hospital earlier that day. She was scheduled to have a Cesarean section to deliver my new baby brother or sister. Sometime early Saturday morning, Dad went back to the hospital to be with her, and then I got the call.

Three hours later, I was on the lawn pushing my old baby carriage when Dad pulled into the driveway. He didn't look very happy and his face was pale. I asked where they were because I had the carriage ready for my brother. He managed a smile and tousled my hair saying they'd be home in a couple of days. Then he went in the house to talk to Oma. Because she was very hard of hearing, even with a hearing aid, he had to speak in a loud voice that I could hear outside. From what I gathered, there was problem with the delivery and my brother didn't look normal and they both would be in the hospital for about a week. I went in to get more information but Dad was on the phone calling the New York relatives to tell them the news. Standing in the dining room, I heard everything he said and apparently something called an umbilical cord had been wrapped around the baby's neck, meaning he didn't get enough oxygen and there was a fear of brain damage. That didn't sound good. In fact, the idea of a cord around the neck reminded me of a story I heard on the radio program, *Gang Busters*, about a crook who tried to strangle a guy with a rope and then rob him. I couldn't understand who would put a rope around my baby brother's neck. This hospital, I surmised, must be full of rogue psychos. If only I had J. Edgar Hoover's phone number, I'd have turned them in and probably collected a handsome reward.

After all the calls, Dad went to the screened porch and stood looking out at the woods. I came up to him and asked what my brother's name was. He lit a cigarette and said my mother liked Robert for a first name and Walter, in honor of Mom's cousin Walter Vogel, would be his middle name. Robert

Walter sounded rather formal to me, but I guessed I could get used to it. "And she insists his name is Robert, not Bob or Bobby," he added.

So every day for the next week, Dad went to the hospital in the morning and headed off to work at the AO in the afternoon. I kept asking when I could see my new brother, but he said no children under sixteen were admitted to the maternity ward. Finally, after four days of pestering, he took me with him to the hospital and told me to stand on the street and watch a window on the third floor, which he pointed out. He went inside and, 10 minutes later, Mom appeared at the window, waving and then holding up a tiny baby. It was Robert. What I remember most about him was how pink he looked. For an instant, I thought there was a mistake and she was holding a baby girl because I knew girls were always depicted as pink.

On the way home I expressed my concern about the pinkness and Dad said all new babies were pink because they hadn't been in the sun yet and hadn't had a chance to get a tan. Made sense to me.

Several days later, Mom and Robert came home. But there was an air of unrest in the house. Mom cried a lot and Robert didn't move around much in his bassinet. Or at least, not the way I thought a baby would. On TV, babies seemed to be all arms and legs and they cried a lot. Our baby just seemed to lie there and not make much noise at all.

My mother's crying continued and would begin for no apparent reason. She would just start to sob, and no amount of consoling comforted her. It was at this time when her hands developed a serious rash. Her hands were red with ugly, open cracks at her knuckles and between her fingers. She said her hands itched like crazy and felt as if they were on fire at the same time. It reminded me of the worst case of poison ivy I ever had, except she hadn't been near any poison ivy. A skin doctor prescribed a gooey white salve, but it didn't help, and she had to wear thick rubber gloves to touch anything.

Meanwhile, Robert didn't move much and barely uttered a sound.

The summer quickly became the fall and Robert was taken to one doctor after another in an effort to determine what was wrong with him. The last one they went to summed up the situation in a detached and succinct way. The umbilical cord around his neck had nothing to do with Robert's condition. He had Down syndrome, or, as the doctor said coldly, he was a mongoloid, a condition likely brought on because Mom was over forty. My parents were stunned. The doctor went on to say there wasn't anything that could be done to help him: he would have poor muscle tone, might never learn to walk, and the good thing was that he would probably die at a very early age. In fact, the doctor advised them to leave Robert in a room without food and he'd be gone in no time, lifting the burden from their lives. So much for compassionate medical care in 1951.

They left that day, determined to prove that doctor wrong and to provide a loving, supportive home for Robert, where he could grow strong and live a normal life.

Joan Malloy was not only our source for Irish Sweepstakes tickets but could also deliver an array of medical procedures that would probably be frowned upon by the American Medical Association. Nonetheless, everything Joan produced had been blessed by a priest and, according to her, that made it better than anything the AMA suggested or was sold in a drugstore. At the end of September she appeared with a suitcase-full of Papal-approved potions and began dispensing them to Mom.

Surprisingly, two such treatments she brought to New Hampshire seemed to work. One was a honey-colored ointment for my mother's hands. As with all of Joan's cures, there was a prayer that needed to be directed to a specific saint for it to work. Praying to Catholic saints was not something we Lutheran/Methodists put much stock in, but Joan swore it worked, and said she could produce hundreds of success stories from people who had been helped. The old man summed up the situation by quoting something a friend from Brooklyn used at times of uncertainty: "It can't hoit."

Within days of Mom's using the stuff, her hands began to heal. Joan said it was important to heal her first so she would be able to touch Robert with her bare hands and administer an oil to make his muscles stronger. A mother's touch is very important, she stressed.

One of Robert's problems was his inability to raise his head. Put a baby on his stomach and he raises his head and looks around, not unlike a turtle peeking out of its shell. But Robert couldn't do that. That's why Joan produced a small bottle of clear oil. It had a slightly sweet smell and she said her parish priest, Father Ryan, procured it from a Catholic doctor who assured him it was blessed by none other than Bishop Fulton J. Sheen himself. Whoa. We were impressed. You didn't need to be Catholic to know that he was the voice of a very popular radio program called *The Catholic Hour*. And even in the wilds of New Hampshire, we had seen him on his one-man show, *Life is Worth Living*. This was big-time stuff.

Accompanying the oil was a small sheet of instructions on how to work it into the baby's weak muscles, along with the prayer that had to be said when doing this. And so it began, twice-a-day applications of the blessed oil rubbed into Robert's neck and shoulders. Joan assured us it would work, and when we needed more she'd send another bottle – special delivery.

Within a few months, Robert was starting to lift his head and he smiled more, behaving the way a baby his age should behave. Now in all honesty, there have been those who, having heard this story, scoffed, and dismissed the oily prayers and their significance. They've said the oil was probably nothing more than drugstore-variety baby oil. One skeptic went to far as to say Mom could have used Crisco with the same results. After all, they said, it was the massaging that really worked by stimulating blood flow and aiding the muscle development. Maybe. But Mom believed the prayers, and the Bishop Sheen blessing did the trick.

Years later, when she would tell this story, she included the comments of the doubters by saying everyone is entitled to their opinion, but then she always added a little anecdote about the power of the good bishop. She would point out that he was very much against Communism in general, and Russian dictator Josef Stalin in particular. And on his television program in 1953, Sheen did a dramatic reading of the burial scene from Shakespeare's *Julius Caesar* – only he substituted the names of Stalin and those around him for Caesar, Cassius, Mark Antony and Brutus. The bishop boldly stated that Stalin must one day meet his judgment. Just a week later, Stalin was dead from a stroke. Smiling, Mom would usually say, "Let's see Crisco do that."

Most children begin to walk at the age of one or so, but Robert didn't take his first solo steps until he was four. Summer people were always eager to help, and someone came up with the idea to put colored pipes in the ground and tell Robert to walk to the red one, then the blue one, then the green one. At first, he would hold onto one pipe in order to reach the next. After a day of this, the pipes were moved several inches farther apart so Robert had to actually take steps – without touching anything – to reach the next pipe. It was a super idea, and over the summer of 1955 he learned to walk on his own, no pipes needed, thank you.

The next big event for Robert came in 1957 when he turned six. The law in New Hampshire said all six-year-olds must attend school. These were the days before home-schooling, so Robert had to start his education. But there was a problem. At that time, New Hampshire didn't have an adequate way to educate children with special needs. To just toss them into a regular first grade class would be unfair to the child, the teacher and the rest of the class. So the

Korradi family was faced with a dilemma.

A celebrated painting by Norman Rockwell from the 1940s is entitled "Freedom of Speech." It is the first of his famous "Four Freedoms" paintings for *The Saturday Evening Post*. In "Speech," a farmer is speaking his mind during the most New England of New England institutions – the town meeting. The painting clearly shows a meeting agenda held in the hand of a man obviously not accustomed to public speaking. He's looking up at a farmer. I have always envisioned my father as that man.

Although New Hampshire was lacking in school facilities for disabled students, neighboring Vermont was ahead of the curve. And Spofford was just ten miles from Brattleboro, Vermont, where the Frances Hicks Memorial School educated special-needs children. However, education money from New Hampshire could not flow to Vermont unless a New Hampshire town agreed to pay for the services. That's

The family in 1955. From left to right: Rover, Oma, Mom, Dad with Robert on his knee, and me in the back.

104

where my dad came in. He and Mom found the Hicks School and they agreed to take Robert if Chesterfield would divert New Hampshire education money to Vermont to pay for his education. To make that happen, Dad had to convince the town selectmen to pony up the bucks. That presentation would occur on Town Meeting Day.

Town Meeting Day is a form of local government that dates its origin in New England to colonial times. In general, it is a chance for residents of the town or school district to gather once a year, usually in March, to voice their opinion on operating budgets, laws and other matters for the community's operation planned for the upcoming twelve months. So Dad would be facing the selectmen, who controlled the town budget, and convincing them to pay for Robert's enrollment in Vermont.

The night before the meeting, he and Mom wrote out their argument on a page of lined paper from one of my school notebooks. His points were simple and straightforward. Lacking a high school, the town of Chesterfield paid for its students to go to Keene or Brattleboro so there was precedent for New Hampshire education money going to Vermont. And even though the town of Chesterfield was proud of a new consolidated elementary school for the residents of the villages of Spofford, Chesterfield and West Chesterfield, its curriculum was not geared for a disabled child. The Hicks School, which would meet Robert's educational requirements, was the perfect answer.

The next day was blustery and cold, perfect for heated debates and pointed discussions. The old man was nervous but tried not to let it show. I was kept out of school so we could appear as a family delegation with Robert as exhibit A.

The Chesterfield town hall was a stone building with hardwood floors and had been used throughout the years for receptions, Boy Scout meetings, dances, and fundraising suppers. But on Town Meeting Day, it was always packed to the rafters as all citizens had the opportunity to express their opinion about issues that would directly affect them. In other words, the proceedings could drag on and on. However, this day the more loquacious either didn't show up, or they agreed with the points the selectmen were presenting so there was little opposition to anything. About an hour into the day's proceedings, the school budget was up for discussion and it was Dad's turn to request funds for Robert's education.

As I have said, even though it was the 1950s, in many respects these were dark ages for children with disabilities and learning problems. Just a few years before this, I had witnessed a shocking event in my own classroom. At the time, there were three two-room schoolhouses in Chesterfield – one for each village. Each room held four grades and each grade had its own row of desks. When the teacher was working with one grade, all the other students were expected to read or study lessons that they would be quizzed on soon. At the time, I was in the third grade row and to my right were the kids in the second grade. One of them, Bernard, was hard of hearing. Truth be known, he was probably deaf because his speech was hard to understand and everyone had to really yell at him before he grasped anything. Everyone included the teacher, who was not as patient as she might have been. Bernard came from a poor family, and I'm sure even the most basic of hearing aids was beyond their financial reach.

On this particular day, Bernard was experiencing a lot of difficulty understanding the teacher who raised her voice in waves of decibels to try to get through to him. Meanwhile, the other kids in the room were beginning to become restless and, to silence them, she slammed her hand on Bernard's desk and screamed, "Shut up, all of you!" This startled Bernard and he started to cry, buried his head in his hands and sobbed uncontrollably. The teacher pounded the desk again, so hard this time Bernard's books jumped and then slid to the floor in a slagheap of pages. This did not help matters. By now, the room was out of control and one kid ran across the hall to get Bernard's older sister, Linda, who was in the seventh grade. Linda and her teacher rushed into the room and they tried to console Bernard but he was hysterical and crying uncontrollably. It was no use.

From that day forward, some kids tried to help Bernard understand things while others picked on him and made monkey sounds when he tried to speak. The odd thing was, up to that moment, I didn't realize there was anything wrong with him. I just thought he was shy and didn't have much to say. That day changed everyone's life in the little schoolroom and, thinking back on it, I guess I understood why my parents didn't want Robert exposed to an atmosphere like that.

So, there we were in the midst of the town meeting, and during the discussion of the school budget, Dad stood and asked permission to speak. Mom was sitting to his left with Robert on her lap and I was next to her. The

Robert's graduation from the Hicks School was a proud moment for our family.

old man was given the nod and, pulling the notes from his shirt pocket, glanced at them as he laid out why the town should pay for Robert to attend the Hicks School. And then it was over. The selectmen conferred briefly and gave their approval without any dissent. My mother started to cry, Robert

107

clapped his hands, and I wondered if this early end to the meeting meant I would have to go back to school that day.

With every bit of good news there is not-so-good news and, although the town okayed paying for Robert's schooling, we had to provide his transportation. Starting in September Mom and Dad did two trips a day to Brattleboro: one to deliver Robert and one bring him home. The old man rode to the AO with a co-worker, and Mom had to learn how to drive to make the afternoon pickup. But they did what needed to be done, in good weather and bad, to see that Robert got the schooling he deserved.

Finally, on June 9, 1970, he graduated from the Hicks School. It was a proud day for our family. My parents' belief in their son, that he deserved the same opportunities afforded every child, had been fulfilled. After graduating, Robert got a job. He continues to work sixty-one years after his birth. For those who thought his life would never amount to anything, Robert proved them wrong. He loves to read, has a keen sense of humor, and enjoys eggnog ice cream, the Three Stooges and John Wayne movies. All in all, that seems pretty normal to me.

LIFE AFTER THE SUMMER PEOPLE

or

Throw Another Epilogue on the Fire

BY 1960, HOSTING SUMMER PEOPLE had just about ended at The Maples. Tourist tastes had changed and fewer people were willing to stay in a private home and share facilities with strangers. New highways and the emergence of amenity-packed roadside motels and hotels also took their toll on The Maples. In addition, 1960 was the year I graduated high school and set off to make something of myself, a continuing work in progress, I might add.

Just three years prior the Russians had launched Sputnik, the first Earth-orbiting artificial satellite that ushered in the space race. The United States was suddenly considered lacking in space technology, and there was a push to emphasize math and science courses to narrow the space gap and for kids to attend college. I, however, was not one of them. Neither of my parents went to college and their attitude, thankfully, was that I should decide what I wanted to do with my life, pursue it in the most effective way possible, and do my very best to be a success.

Radio was an early and continuing influence on my life so I stated that I wanted to be an announcer. I never said I wanted to be like Ozzie Wade, knowing that his penchant for public coffee-slurping would have made my mother cringe, yet his influence was always a part of me. My high school guidance counselor suggested I look into Emerson College in Boston or the University of Florida as two excellent schools where I could get a degree in broadcast communications. I had to tell her that I really wasn't interested in a degree in anything; I just wanted to get on the radio as soon as possible, play the hits and say wise-ass things. She shook her head and reluctantly directed me to the Cambridge School of Broadcasting in Boston, a one-year school that would set me on my career path as quickly as possible.

In fact, I had already started down the boulevard of

What am I laughing about? My first paid radio job at WTSA in Brattleboro, Vermont. I took home $50 a week and all the duplicate records I could carry. But it was showbiz, baby, showbiz!

broadcasting by winning a disc-jockey-for-a-day contest at a record hop sponsored by WKBK in Keene. With my foot in the door, I convinced the program director to let me read news headlines on weekend afternoons so the disc jockeys could take a break from their broadcast chores. WKBK was the new radio kid in town. It played all the latest rock 'n' roll records and I envisioned it as my ticket to stardom.

This was a time when stations had to do newscasts every hour and because there were no news announcers who worked weekends, the DJs had to spin records and read the news, too. It could make for a very long shift without any breaks, but I volunteered to do it for free in exchange for the experience. The word "free" appealed to the program director and he agreed. God bless him, because I was awful.

My first day "on the air" was in the spring of 1960 and the breaking news was a crisis in Africa centered on the Congo's fight for independence from Belgium. I'm sure it didn't mean much to the flinty citizens of New Hampshire, but the Associated Press led every five-minute news summary with the story, and that meant I had to read it. What a nightmare! Every dispatch contained names I had no idea how to pronounce correctly. Names such as Joseph Kasa-Vubu, Patrice Émery Lumumba, Dag Hammarskjöld, Kisangani province, and my personal favorite, Moise Tshombé. After stumbling through those a few times, I realized why Ozzie slurped coffee and left the heavy lifting of news reading to the CBS Radio Network. But WKBK didn't have a network option and on summer weekends, it was yours truly. I'm sure everyone listening wanted to hear more rock 'n' roll and I couldn't blame them. I didn't want to hear any more of those screwy names or even my own voice, but I was looking for experience and that's what I got.

In September I started school in Boston and it was everything I dreamed it would be. I learned how to run control boards, edit tape, write commercials, create sound effects and, most importantly, how to overcome my very New England accent.

John Kennedy had just become president, and although his New England way of speaking was considered quaint and appealing by many, it wasn't acceptable for radio announcers, especially if they hoped to work in New York or some other exotic location where a New England burr would have stuck out like the proverbial sore thumb. JFK had a habit of putting "er" on words that ended in "a". So when he said America it came out *Americer*, Cuba became *Cuber* and India was *Indier*. Who was going to correct the president of the United States? No one. But my instructors reprimanded me every day to get it right. And eventually I did.

Broadcasting live from Canada, where there were more sled dogs and seals than people watching the news.

By March of 1961, I was itching to start working and, after sending out dozens of audition tapes I landed my first real, paying radio gig at WTSA in Brattleboro, Vermont. As fate would have it, I was only 10 miles from home, so I moved back into my old room, except now the old man said because I was working, I'd have to pay for the privilege of living there. Suddenly, I had become one of the summer people.

WTSA was my springboard to a long and rewarding career in broadcasting and advertising. In the early 1980s there was a hit TV sitcom about a radio station, *WKRP in Cincinnati.* The theme song had a line in it about "livin' life up and down the dial." That summed up my life in broadcasting: I went from being just a disc jockey to program director to TV news anchor and then general manager of many stations. From Brattleboro to Albany, New York, to Springfield, Massachusetts, to Omaha, Nebraska, to Syracuse, New York, to Norfolk, Virginia, to small towns in New Hampshire and Connecticut, with stops in Canada and four years with the

United States Air Force and the Armed Forces Radio and Television Service, life was one new set of call letters after another. A couple of marriages and divorces along the way, and a lot of crazy characters have all added humor, color, and adventure to my life.

ROVER WAS HIT by a car in 1959, Oma died in 1967, Dad in 1991, and Mom in 1999 at the age of 90. Creating this collection of true stories has allowed me to look back and reflect on a sweeter, less complicated time. I owe all of the summer people a great deal of thanks for their presence in my life. Some were wild, some were wacky, but all were memorable. Thank you, summer people.

EPILOGUE REDUX

AS I WRITE THIS it is July 2, 2016, and Robert has been dead for nine months to the day.

Early in the morning back on October 2, 2015, I received a call from the care facility where he was staying telling me he had passed away. I was devastated and still am. It has taken me this long to sum up the courage and the words to conclude this story.

Officially, my brother Robert died of pneumonia brought on by Alzheimer's. The final three weeks of his life were not kind and he did not deserve the torment he endured. Nor does anyone who has to face that disease.

Yet through it all he smiled up to the end, and the last time I saw him he hugged me and said he would see me tomorrow. For Robert, tomorrow never came.

I am richer for having had him in my life for 64 years. Robert was my wealth and now I am a pauper. He lit up every room with a grin that melted the hardest heart. His way off-key singing of hymns in church every Sunday brought smiles to the faithful and more than one person would say, "Robert, you sounded good today." To which he would beam and reply, "Oh, thank you." He was nothing if not polite, a tribute to our parents and their guidance.

And so the story ends. What doesn't end is how very much I miss him. I miss his laugh, his humor and the quirky way he would say things. I miss him every day in ways that can never be put into words. Odd that I should say that, being a journeyman wordsmith, but it is true.

This is how I remember him: my good pal and my sweet little brother.

The Korradi boys: too cool for the room.

www.ingramcontent.com/pod-product-compliance
Lightning Source LLC
Chambersburg PA
CBHW031340040426
42443CB00006B/417